PRAISE FOR ASPIRE TO LEAD

Becoming a leader in a school or district can be a difficult journey, especially if you don't have guidance in the process. In *Aspire to Lead*, Joshua Stamper uses his own experiences and expertise to provide a framework of relevant steps to direct and inspire growth. No matter your profession or your goals, this book will help you navigate through the adversity of leadership, while reminding you to be empathetic, creative, and passionate in the process. This is a wonderful resource and will have a profound impact on future and current leaders.

— **THOMAS C. MURRAY**, DIRECTOR OF INNOVATION, FUTURE READY SCHOOLS, AUTHOR OF BEST-SELLER, *PERSONAL & AUTHENTIC: DESIGNING LEARNING EXPERIENCES THAT IMPACT A LIFETIME*

Driven, devoted, and passionate - all words that perfectly describe Joshua Stamper on his leadership journey. Inspired by honest and impactful stories of hard lessons and valuable insights learned, not only aspiring leaders but all leaders will walk away better equipped to continue on their own leadership pathway. Joshua's ASPIRE model is a motivational roadmap to follow on your personal route to accomplish goals. An inspirational book with practical ideas and invitations to take action towards growth - a must-read!

— **LIVIA CHAN**, ELEMENTARY HEAD TEACHER, AUTHOR, DIGITAL CONTENT EDITOR FOR THE TEACH BETTER TEAM

An inspiring and empowering call to action! With a deep appreciation for the emotional side of leadership, readers are guided through the ASPIRE model to improve their practice and propel themselves to the next level. Leveraging his own experiences as well as the experiences of his peers, Joshua Stamper illustrates service with empathy, passion, and creativity. If you are ready to evolve in your leadership journey, this book is required reading!

— **LAINIE ROWELL,** LEAD AUTHOR OF EVOLVING
LEARNER AND INTERNATIONAL EDUCATION
CONSULTANT

Whether you're new to education, an aspiring school leader, or simply on your educator journey, I highly recommend you read *ASPIRE to Lead.* Joshua Stamper tells his story from the place of humility—his statement, "I'm not the hero of the story," allows readers to be comfortable with productive struggle and the growing pains required for natural but progressive growth. Leading very early on in the book with the ASPIRE Model and then unpacking each element in subsequent chapters provides readers the necessary guidance wherever they may be in their leadership journey. Bravo—Joshua hits a grand slam with his first book. I can't wait to see what's next!

— **JORGE VALENZUELA,** EDUCATION COACH,
AUTHOR, ADVOCATE

Aspire to Lead is a must-read book for school and district leaders. This is the book we've been waiting for on how to lead productive change that embodies the premise that educational leaders need to model what we want to see in the classrooms. Joshua Stamper takes the reader on a journey that enhances their leadership capacity. Each chapter offers a path that weaves personal stories with stories from practitioners in the field, along with useful strategies and practical calls to action. I highly recommend leaders and those aspiring to lead to keep this book close. If you don't have the answers now, this book gives you the right questions to ask and the guidance you need when you need it.

— **BARBARA BRAY**, CREATIVE LEARNING
STRATEGIST, PODCAST HOST, SPEAKER, AUTHOR
OF *DEFINE YOUR WHY*

Aspire to Lead is an inspiring and practical guide to the ongoing and reflective work it takes to grow as a leader. In reflecting on his own educational and leadership journey, Joshua Stamper vulnerably and powerfully shares key insight and advice for anyone seeking a leadership position in education - and he makes it clear: if you work in a school, you are a leader. *Aspire to Lead* will remind you to lead with empathy and to foster relationships so that you can make a positive and significant difference no matter the role you play in your school or organization.

— **GREG MOFFITT**, ELEMENTARY PRINCIPAL

We know that reflections are key to breakthroughs along with epiphanies we've gleaned. *Aspire To Lead* is one of those books that illuminates the way forward. I've been in education in different roles for what is approaching two decades, and I can tell you that Joshua is the real deal. Simply stated, you need to get this book immediately. It's time to make that move!

— **VERNON WRIGHT**, LEADER, SPEAKER, CONSULTANT, LIFE COACH, FOUNDER

Joshua Stamper's book, *Aspire to Lead*, is so much more than a guide for aspiring administrators. It reads like an autobiography. The reader becomes engrossed in Joshua's story, feeling as if they are also on the same aspiring school administrator journey. We feel his pains, cheer throughout his triumphs, and want nothing more than to see Joshua meet his goal. After walking in Joshua's shoes, we come across sage advice to become a better leader and steps towards acquiring our dream administrative position. *Aspire to Lead* will help not only those seeking to make the leap into school administration, but even seasoned veterans to self-reflect on their own practice. The advice and suggestions in Joshua's book work, not through years of research and analysis, but through first-hand experience. Give *Aspire to Lead* a read and become the administrator your staff, families, and students deserve.

— **MICHAEL EARNSHAW**, PRINCIPAL, AUTHOR, PODCASTER, SPEAKER

I have looked to Joshua for wisdom and perspective on the topic of school leadership as a longtime Aspire: The Leadership Development Podcast listener. I have always found Joshua's voice to be authentic, kind, and compassionate. He has transferred his inspiring podcast to a book that is just as spectacular. This book outlines the path to a school leadership position. It traces Josh's journey through the lens of the ASPIRE Model action steps providing gems of advice and support along the way. There are equal parts inspirational moments and practical advice with personal examples from Joshua and other contributing authors. The guest author statements are from experienced, influential, reflective leaders who generously offer advice, insight, and support. Joshua answers his own introductory podcast prompt, "Tell me about your leadership journey," with his honesty and vulnerability. In exposing his heart for leading those within his charge, we will all benefit and aspire to become better leaders.

— **MICHELLE PAPA**, PRINCIPAL AT RICHARD
BUTLER MIDDLE SCHOOL

#AspireLead

Thank you for all you do for your Students, Parents, & community!.

ASPIRE TO LEAD

JOSHUA STAMPER

EduMatch
PUBLISHING

ISBN: 978-1-953852-38-0

This book is dedicated to the love of my life, Leslie Stamper. Being married to you has been the greatest blessing and honor. Thank you for always believing in me and pushing me to be better each day.

CONTENTS

FOREWORD

BY TODD NESLONEY

When Joshua asked me to write the foreword to his book, I was floored. Having never written a foreword, I didn't even know where I would begin. Then I thought about the forewords that I have enjoyed reading before jumping into some of my favorite books. They're filled with hope, honesty, and a little preview of what's to come.

I've been able to get to know Joshua quite well over the last few years and one thing that is clear from the moment you interact with him is his immense passion for helping others. When he told me he was writing this book, I was beyond excited not only for him but for all of you. Every single conversation I've ever had with Joshua, I've left as a better educator, leader, and person.

Though I knew who Joshua was from my personal interactions with him, I still didn't quite expect this book to move me as much as it did.

I've had the extreme pleasure of serving as a classroom teacher and then feeling the tug of a larger leadership role. After getting my master's, I was afforded the opportunity to go straight from classroom teacher to elementary school principal. The ride was wild, and I only wished that there were more books like Joshua's to help me navigate the new role I was inhabiting. As I've entered into my current role as a Director at TEPSA, this book has given me even more tools in my tool chest.

Even now, after seven years in a leadership role outside the classroom, there were multiple takeaways for me from this book. But I think the biggest things I walked away with were the reminders of how we all have leadership within us and that leadership looks different on everyone.

You see, leadership isn't about just a fancy title or a new office. Leadership is something that is a very personal journey that we all experience differently. But that's exactly what this book does. It teaches you how to persevere through even the most challenging situations. It helps you learn the power of reflection and how to utilize that reflection to grow into a better overall person. It gives you all the tools necessary to become the leader anyone would be willing to follow, regardless of your title.

But a book can only do so much. Joshua has written something that gives you every tool you could need to achieve success as a leader. But YOU have to take that first step. You have to take the risks, prepare for the failures, and ready yourself to keep going. This book is the perfect way to begin or continue that personal journey.

Leadership doesn't have one particular path for success. But by picking up and reading this book, you've taken a powerful step in the right direction. One that changed me, and I'm pretty sure will change you too.

INTRODUCTION

> *"Everyone is smart in different ways. But if you judge a fish on its ability to climb a tree, it will spend its whole life thinking that it's stupid."*
>
> — *LYNDA MULLALY HUNT, "FISH IN A TREE"*

s a student, my perspective of education was extremely negative. I often experienced unsuccessfulness in an established learning environment. From my adolescent view, the school was a mandatory placement where the material, procedures, and system provided little value. The presented content was often detached from a real-world application, classes were teacher-directed, differentiation rarely occurred, retesting and late work were not allowed, and the classroom setup wasn't conducive to many individual learning styles. As a traditional system, there were few opportunities for recovery, and I found myself doubting my ability as a learner, which led to a dismissive and uninspired work ethic. Similar to the metaphor, I felt like a fish trying to climb a tree. All I wanted to do was move around, use my imagination, and create new things. Instead, I was asked to sit down, memorize facts, and regurgitate information. The only reason I got out of bed and went to school was due to my love of art class and athletics. Those classes were the joy of my day and I couldn't wait to be creative and compete.

As you can probably guess, my grades in my other classes were not stellar and my teachers and parents were constantly frustrated by my decisions. I often received lectures on the importance of school. Parent and teacher conferences consisted of the same phrases to describe my progress:

- Shows a lack of effort in the class.
- Does not apply himself.
- Disorganized, loses his work, and doesn't complete his homework.
- Has the potential to do well in the class.

I realized it was easier to not try than to risk my energy and effort on potential failure in the classroom. The low marks on tests and homework did not motivate me. I began to boast about my failing grades to my peers and I loved controlling the narrative of "not caring." In my mind, attending school was a giant waste of my time and I wasn't going to use the majority of what I was learning when I became an adult.

RUDE AWAKENING

During high school, many students were looking at college and deciding where they were going to enroll. Plans beyond high school were not a priority to me. In the back of my mind, I figured college would be an option once I graduated but I had serious reservations about continuing my education. Unfortunately, my grades didn't reflect college readiness and I didn't have any real plan for my educational future. My tactic was to ignore the problem as long as I possibly could.

Toward the beginning of my senior year, I was called into the counselor's office to discuss my grades and my future. The meeting was standard for every senior and involved a one-on-one meeting with our guidance counselor. My counselor, Mr. Lake, displayed my grades on a table, while he asked me if I wanted to go to college. As I looked at my grades, I was disappointed to see several pages littered with low marks.

With no plan for my future in mind, I said, "Yes."

Mr. Lake was surprised by my answer. He responded with, "What college do you want to go to?"

Quickly, I responded, "Bethel College." I knew exactly where I wanted to go because my mentor and youth pastor went to this college. As a youth group, we attended several events there and I absolutely fell in love with the campus.

It was obvious by Mr. Lake's face that he found my response annoyingly unrealistic. He knew I had never researched any requirements for acceptance into the college.

Suddenly, his tone of voice changed and he began to quickly ask questions.

"Do you know what grades you would need to be accepted by Bethel College? Have you taken an ACT or SAT exam? Do you know how much it costs to go to a private college?"

The questions came so fast that I didn't have a chance to answer each one. I interrupted his line of questioning by explaining that during the summer, I visited the campus and I enjoyed the experience.

Mr. Lake looked agitated by my response and, while dramatically pointing at my high school transcripts, he said, "You will never get into college. Not a state college or a community college. You will not get into a private college and, especially, not Bethel College!"

I got up and left Mr. Lake's office extremely angry. Although the conversation lacked tact, the meeting created a burning drive and desire to prove the negative perception of my abilities as incorrect. The strong emotions produced by this experience created an unstoppable intrinsic motivation that still exists today. I was determined to show him that I was capable of learning and to show everyone that I was more than a grade. From that point on, it was my mission to go to college. But not any college; I wanted to prove to him that I was going to go to the college of my choice.

CHALLENGE ACCEPTED

After meeting with my guidance counselor, I made the mental shift to work harder and to apply myself in my learning. My goal was to improve my grades, increase my GPA, and gain an acceptable ACT score. That year, although my grades improved, my ACT score was below the number accepted by private colleges. I submitted my application to Bethel and another in-state private college, but I knew my odds were low to be accepted.

A couple of months later, I received several letters from colleges explaining that I was not accepted into their institutions. Each time I opened a denial letter, I felt defeated by the weight of my prior decisions. Of all of the letters, the denial letter from Bethel College was the hardest to read. As my mother consoled me, she asked me to read the letter to her. When I read the letter, she got excited and showed me the bottom of the letter. It stated that if I did not agree with the college's decision, I could appeal the denial. I immediately began writing the letter of appeal and I sent it to the college. That summer, after my high school gradua-tion, I received a letter from the college asking for me to come to the campus for a meeting.

When I arrived at the campus, they asked me to come to a board room, where six people were sitting at a long table. I sat down on one end of the table and they sat on the other side. They began asking me a variety of questions on why I thought I should be allowed to enroll at Bethel College and why my grades were so low as a freshman and sophomore in high school. I explained how I didn't enjoy school and I didn't apply myself early in my high school career. It wasn't until I visited colleges that I realized I needed to start improving my grades to obtain the opportunity to further my education. Although I was extremely nervous, the committee was great about making me feel comfortable and they were truly trying to understand my story. After the meeting was complete, I was asked to wait outside with my family. A woman appeared and asked how I thought the meeting went. I was so nervous that I didn't really know how to answer the question. She then asked if I was ready to be a student at Bethel College. At first, I couldn't believe it but once it set in, I felt immense joy. I was placed on academic probation for my freshman year, but I didn't care. I had obtained my goal and I wasn't going to lose this opportunity.

UNEXPECTED CHANGE

The beginning of my freshman year in college was a giant learning curve, but I adapted quickly. I played on the school's soccer team and at the end of my freshman season, our coach announced that our team had the opportunity to travel to Sweden that upcoming summer. We immediately started raising funds for the trip. As a team, each weekend, we cleaned a local university hockey rink and divided the check equally among each of us. One evening after cleaning the hockey stadium, I came home for a weekend visit. When I walked through the door, I heard my mom crying on the living room couch.

"What's wrong, mom?"

She responded, "Your dad is gone. He left and I don't think he is coming back."

I knew my parents were having a difficult time but they had always found a way to work things out. This time it felt different, and I knew things were never going to be the same. My anger engulfed me and I quickly left the house to go back to my college campus. After that evening, my motivation to get out of bed, go to class, and be successful was gone. Most days, I tried every way possible to ignore my feelings and my school work. My grades were slipping and I was just trying to get through the duration of the semester.

After I completed my freshman year, I went home and lived with my mom for the summer. One summer morning, my mom came down to the basement and told me I had a letter from my college. Suddenly, my heart stopped and I ran and grabbed the letter. The letter stated that I did not meet the GPA requirements to stay enrolled at Bethel College. I thought I was going to throw up. I quickly scanned my grades to find that I failed my physics course, which caused my GPA to plummet. When I told my mom, her face dropped and she said, "You are going to need to figure this out." The way she said it and walked away, it cut right through me. I realized that I squandered the largest opportunity of my life and I may not have another chance to redeem myself. Once again, I wrote a letter to the college to appeal their decision.

When I went in front of the campus board for a second time, the feeling in the room was very different. Their faces were longer, the questions were very pointed, and they never cracked a smile. I shared what had happened with my family during the school year, the plan I had moving forward to be successful, and the many reasons why I wanted to stay at the school. When I left the meeting, my mom stood up quickly from the hallway bench.

She asked, "How did it go?"

I said, "I didn't get back in."

She was shocked and asked, "They said that?"

Crushed by the experience, I said, "No, mom, I just know."

As I walked out of the doors, I thought it was going to be the last time I set foot on Bethel's campus. A week later, I received a letter from the college. In my mind, I had already prepared myself to either work full time or go to the local community college. When I read the letter, tears began to roll down my face. I was re-enrolled at Bethel College. The admittance was for one semester, and I had to achieve a designated minimum grade point average for the semester, see a school counselor once a week, and was suspended from playing soccer for one season. I knew I couldn't take this opportunity for granted.

> "One word of encouragement can be enough
> to spark someone's motivation to continue
> with a difficult challenge."
> ~ Roy T. Bennett

ENCOURAGEMENT IS ALWAYS NEEDED

It was obvious my sophomore year was my last chance to get my college career back on track. The first person to help me get through this tough time with my family was a college professor. One morning, he asked me to stay after class. I figured he was going to scold me for my lack of effort.

He calmly sat down next to me and asked, "Are you on drugs?"

"What? No!" I said as I began to laugh.

My professor did not laugh. He was concerned about my lack of effort and wanted to know how he could help me. I told him about what was going on at home and how I was on academic probation. Instead of yelling at me, he told me he believed in my artistic skills and he challenged me to lead a class activity on painting techniques to begin class the following day. I was shocked that his response was grounded in support and not disappointment in my previous decisions. Instead of blowing off the request, I accepted the challenge. The time he spent inquiring about my life, which only took a few minutes, encouraged me to take steps toward reconciliation. As soon as I got home that afternoon, I prepared the art activity for the next day's class. With his challenge and belief in my leadership skills, my confidence was boosted and propelled me to take command of my current situation.

This conversation and the relationship that was established with my professor was the turning point of my educational career. I had a lot of self-doubt about my abilities as a student and I didn't know if I could rise to the occasion. The professors, my peers, and my family continued to encourage me until I realized that I had the ability to succeed.

With each school year, I became more successful in my studies. My senior year in college was when I began my leadership journey. I was voted to be co-captain of my college soccer team and asked to be the co-leader of a leadership development program. The leadership development program was the transition from sports to leading in other capacities. I really enjoyed the experience and challenge of developing future leaders and knew I wanted to continue to lead in some capacity in the future.

FROM ARTIST TO TEACHER

I graduated from Bethel College with a Bachelor's in Art, majoring in Fine Art, and began my career as a graphic designer for a local digital photographer in Minnesota. During my third year of working with the photographer, the economy was very unstable and small businesses were struggling to stay open. I was informed that the company was losing money and my position was going to be dissolved. I remember driving home panicked because I had no clue what I was going to do. With the economy crashing, work was hard to find and I only had a few months to find a new job. My wife, Leslie, was so calm and understanding. We talked through my passions and the profession that correlated to those dreams.

Two months later, I enrolled at Bethel College (now renamed Bethel University) again, this time in their graduate program to obtain my teaching license in Visual Arts for grades K-12. While completing the licensure program, I worked as a soccer coach and a junior high Special Education paraprofessional. My time as a coach and paraprofessional, in correlation with my education courses, was incredible. The experiences obtained helped prepare me to be ready for my first years of teaching. Upon obtaining my certification to teach, I was hired to be a middle school art teacher. I vowed to be the teacher I needed growing up and to identify every student who felt like a fish climbing a tree.

CALL TO ACTION:

- Don't let anyone tell you what you can and cannot do. We are not defined by our mistakes. Instead, we are defined by how we overcome those mistakes. We all fail and will continue to fail in every stage of life. Failure is the most powerful experience in the learning process. If you want to be a college graduate, artist, soccer coach, teacher, or administrator, you will not be given that opportunity without overcoming adversity. Focus on your growth and know that you are capable of obtaining your dreams!

- As an educator, please know that many of the students sitting in your class or walking the halls of your school feel as though they are a fish trying to climb a tree. They may not see the value in school or struggle with an area of their life you can't see. Please take the time to ask them, "How are you doing?" or "How can I help you be more successful?" The relationship with our students is the most important aspect of learning. To get knowledge into the brain, we have to first go through the heart.

PART I

THE A.S.P.I.R.E. MODEL

*"Before you are a leader, success is all about growing yourself.
When you become a leader, success is all about growing others."*

— *JACK WELCH*

One day while walking the campus, I entered a classroom to find one of my team leaders sitting at her desk with her head down. As I got closer, I realized she was crying. When I asked her what was wrong, she explained that she'd had a difficult conversation with a teacher on her academic team.

"I don't think I have what it takes to be a leader. Am I even making a difference? It's not like I'm an administrator."

This teacher was an amazing leader, a hard worker, and a creative educator. But she was questioning her abilities and value to the campus. Over the years, there have been many times that I have had these same thoughts. No matter if you have been a leader for one day or twenty years, self-doubt and fear creep into the picture. Perhaps you struggle with the same questions.

Who is a leader?

I want to establish a norm that you must carry with you, not only as you read this book, but as you continue your journey as a leader. This important concept is often mistaken, especially when this simple question is asked.

In my experience, most teachers, counselors, and administrators answer this question by discussing their leadership titles, awards, and accomplishments.

I am here to tell you, every educator is a leader.

A title, stipend, or pay grade does not make you a leader. If you show up each day to serve all students, colleagues, and community members, you are a leader. A leadership title does not define your impact or influence in the lives of others. In almost twenty years of education, I have seen plenty of people with impressive titles make little to no contributions on their campus or in the lives of those they are supposed to serve. Leaders are determined by their inspiring impact and motivating actions, nothing more.

Becoming an effective leader is a difficult accomplishment and there will be many trials along the way. Similar to my team leader, there will be days you wonder if you are making an impact. This book is a guide, using stories of failure, trials, and perseverance to provide hope, strength, and encouragement in your leadership experience. I hope that my stories allow you to see the challenges ahead so you don't make the same mistakes.

I'M NOT THE HERO OF THE STORY

In the middle of my first year of administration, I was struggling with my role as a leader. I questioned my impact, ability, and purpose in my new position. Overwhelmed and desperate to prove myself, I tried to solve every problem and take on each task alone. In reflection of my actions, I realized I was trying to be the hero.

Throughout my childhood, I was enamored with superheroes, which involved a solid rotation of reading comic books, collecting action figures, and dressing up to save the world from destruction. Every Saturday morning, I would run to the TV to watch old *Batman* reruns, starring Adam West, and *The Amazing Spider-Man* cartoons. The story-lines of possessing extraordinary powers used to rescue others, overcome adversity, and defeat evil were concepts I relished in. Each amazing hero, villainous foe, and unstoppable monster I desperately tried to recreate in my sketchbooks, on loose pieces of paper, and in the margins of class notes.

As my interest in art grew, my only motivation to go to school was to participate in every art class I could. I never wanted to leave the studio. Although my experience in the art classroom was transformational, which I'll discuss later in the book, the rest of my educational career created trepidation, frustration, and uncertainty as a learner. My view of education and the entire system of learning was jaded. When I became an educator, I wanted to be the solution and change education so students like me would find joy instead of hardship.

Later, as a new leader, I took this same "hero mindset" and tried to take on every problem by myself. I attempted to be the hero and with each opportunity, to prove I was going to save the day. After many struggles and feeling overwhelmed and burnt out, I had a realization that struck me. I couldn't do it alone. No one can lead effectively by themselves.

This was difficult to swallow because as a child, I inundated myself with stories of heroes individually conquering endless missions. Yet after years of being a teacher, coach, and administrator, it was evident that leadership is not a one-person mission. As educators, we also possess extraordinary powers to support others, overcome hardships, and identify challenges for our stakeholders. However, we cannot single-handedly redefine, improve, and impact education. It takes many educational leaders to create change. With a shift in my mindset, I established a new mission. My charge turned to guiding and building up new leaders.

You are the leader of your school, district, and community, but you can't do it alone. Together, as a collective whole, we will do great things as you ASPIRE to Lead!

The ASPIRE Model

In this book, I am going to use a circular "ASPIRE Model" to guide you in your leadership journey. Regardless of your experience, this model will assist in accomplishing your goals and creating the greatest impact. The model follows the acronym, A.S.P.I.R.E. (see below), and throughout the book, I will be sharing each step of the ASPIRE Model, which consists of core leadership values, real-world examples, and action steps.

A: Activate

This chapter explains the first step in any process. You have to act. Many people brainstorm great ideas and have the best intentions.

However, if you don't activate yourself, you will not be able to accomplish your goals.

S: Support

Behind every great leader is an amazing mentor. In this chapter, I share the importance and advantages of finding someone to guide and assist in your leadership experience. It doesn't matter how many years you have been a leader; the most important thing you can do is find a mentor to enhance your progression.

P: Persevere

At some point, you are going to fail. Instead of fixating on the immediate result, we need to learn from our mistakes and try again. This chapter explains the steps necessary to fight through the struggles and be victorious in your endeavors.

I: Identify

When you become a leader or change roles, your responsibilities dramatically change. Unfortunately, your position isn't the only thing that changes. The way you are viewed and perceived by your peers evolves quickly too. In this chapter, you will receive a guide on how to embrace your identity as a leader, while identifying the needs of your organization.

R: Reflect

Reflection is one of the most important learning opportunities leaders possess to improve their skills. When you think of reflection, you may find that very little time is designated for this practice. This chapter provides simple steps to designate and utilize your time to process your previous actions.

. . .

E: Execute

Once we have gone through each of the steps in the ASPIRE Model, it is time to execute our plans. The preparation, guidance, and identification are complete and it's time to put the plans to work. This chapter offers insights on how to execute your plans to obtain optimal results while gaining support from your team.

The topics in each chapter will be further developed through inserts by guest authors, action steps, guided questions, and additional resources.

Guest Authors

In my second year as an administrator, I had the opportunity to hear George Couros speak at a local conference. During his presentation, Couros stated, "The smartest person in the room is the room." As an educational leader, it is easy to think you need all the answers to every problem. However, that could not be further from the truth.

In this book, I wanted to bring additional leaders to the table to speak on important leadership topics, provide their personal stories, and share advice to aspiring and current leaders. Each one of these guest authors is a leader and has made a giant impact on my leadership journey. I am so grateful for their willingness to share their insight and wisdom in this book.

Aspire Action Steps

At the end of each chapter, there will be a section called "ASPIRE Action Steps," providing you with some practical suggestions to enhance your leadership journey. It is important to read, study, and learn leadership concepts; however, the most important step in the process is to act. Over my time as an educational leader, I have heard many aspiring leaders talk about moving up to the next level, only to be followed by inactivity and complacency. *Aspire to Lead* will challenge you to go beyond the text. Action creates results.

. . .

Discussion Questions

In connection with the ASPIRE action steps, I want each reader to be able to reflect after each chapter. It's important to spend some time thinking and working through your experiences, choices, and results. We are going to have successes and failures throughout our time as a leader. We need to dissect our decisions and learn from the evidence. Please make sure you have an outlet to reflect. It doesn't have to be complicated, like a blog or a podcast. If you are more comfortable with a sketchbook or journal, use these items to flush out and challenge your thoughts and ideas.

Supporting Material

As an assistant principal, I had the opportunity to build a leadership development group with five other assistant principals. The project was a district pilot program, and as a small group, we designed the program to allow teachers to experience leadership tasks, such as simulated problems, controversial topics, and life-like conversations. The program was so successful that the district adopted it on a larger scale. The following year, I realized that I wanted to continue to have a role in the development of future leaders.

My solution was to create a podcast called *Aspire: The Leadership Development Podcast*. The premise of the podcast was to interview other amazing leaders to gain insight into leadership positions, difficult aspects of the job, and creative strategies, with the goal to inspire aspiring leaders. At the end of each chapter, I will have a QR code for a related podcast as an additional free resource to help expand on the topic at hand.

As you read this book, remember, *leaders don't need to wear a mask or a cape but our students, parents, and community need your superpowers every day!*

1

ASPIRE TO ACTIVATE

 The more you see yourself as what you'd like to become, and act as if what you want is already there, the more you'll activate those dormant forces that will collaborate to transform your dream into your reality.

— WAYNE DYER

START YOUR JOURNEY

*A*fter my third year of teaching, I had the opportunity to be a middle school football, basketball, and track coach. I quickly found that the new role allowed me to impact many students, parents, and staff well beyond my classroom. Coaching created the opportunity to make connections with students on a much deeper level, and I was viewed differently by everyone on campus. My role didn't change just with students. Suddenly, teachers began to utilize my position to assist in their classes and motivate students to do better in their classrooms. After the second month of coaching, I was in the teacher's lounge getting coffee when my assistant principal approached me. He asked how I enjoyed coaching and we discussed how the new role expanded my perspective on the entire campus. He agreed with my view on the new role and then asked me a question that changed my career completely.

"Have you ever considered administration?"

At first, I laughed but then after looking at his face, I quickly realized he was serious. My assistant principal continued to say that there were several teachers in the building trying to complete their administrative certification but he thought I had the potential to be the best candidate to be accepted into the district's administrative pool. The district required teachers to interview to be selected as candidates for the position of Dean of Students. The Dean of Students role was designed to provide administrative experience in student discipline, lockers, keys, facilities, and teacher appraisal. If you did well in the Dean of Students role, you were promoted to assistant principal at a different campus. At the time, I was just getting comfortable being a teacher and a new coach. I had never considered administration and I assumed I had to be teaching for a long time before becoming an assistant principal. My assistant principal told me about the process to obtain a principal certification and encouraged me to enroll in a program. Immediately, my first thought was, *"There is no way the district is going to allow an art teacher to become an administrator."*

It was hard to process the conversation. I immediately spoke to my wife, Leslie, about the possibility of advancing my career and the logistics of continuing education. After much thought, I decided to get additional information about furthering my career in administration and enrolling in a graduate degree program. I felt honored that my assistant principal believed I could become an administrator, but I was afraid of the journey ahead of me. I knew there was going to be a lot of work ahead to make the leap from art teacher to administrator. Despite my fear and apprehension, by the next month, I was enrolled in a Master's program in Educational Administration at Lamar University.

The reason I was tapped on the shoulder by my assistant principal was that he saw I was active beyond my classroom. I was seeking opportunities to help my students in any way I could, such as mentoring students, visiting classrooms, checking student grades, and advocating for my athletes. My impact became larger because I inserted my skills into areas of need and became an active member of the campus. Due to my actions, I was viewed as a quality candidate to become a campus leader.

STRIVE TO BE AN OFFICE RAT

As my Master's program began, the university informed us that we would be conducting an administrative internship throughout the process. We were required to complete leadership tasks, meet with our administrators, and reflect on our practices. Each day during my conference period, I would try to go to the front office to work on any administrative tasks that were required for my program's internship. I would sit down with my assistant principal or principal to discuss the program assignments and ask questions on every aspect of the administrative position. Even when my internship tasks were complete, I went to the front office to learn about administrative practices, observe leadership situations, attend meetings, and get the opportunity to apply my skills to different leadership experiences. Based on my consistent visits to the front office, they began to call me the "office rat." Although the name seems unendearing, it was meant as a compliment. The nickname was saying I was a hungry aspiring leader who was always in the front office. I was longing for more information and I wanted to experience more leadership opportunities.

Every aspiring leader needs to prove they are hungry to grow and strive to be the campus *Office Rat*. Here are some tips on how to become an *Office Rat*:

Knock on the Door

There were plenty of days that the office doors were closed. My belief is, if you don't knock, no one will open the door. Although it may be uncomfortable to ask permission to observe an administrative situation, you have to be persistent. As a new leader, we can't be afraid to ask to experience new and different leadership tasks. A door should not get in the way of the search for growth. Sometimes my administrators said yes and other times they said no. Every time they said yes, I was presented with a quality leadership experience and a new perspective on the job. These opportunities were instrumental in my leadership development and provided me with invaluable knowledge of the position.

Best Ability is Availability

I heard a sportscaster, Jim Benz from Fox Sports North, say, "The best ability is availability." Although Jim was using this statement for a basketball game, it applies to aspiring leaders. One day during my off period, I was walking down the main hall of the campus and realized there was a weird smell. After some investigation from the administrators, it smelled like natural gas on the far side of the building. The students began to complain to their teachers about the smell and stated they felt dizzy. I walked over to my principal and asked how I could help. I was provided a portable radio and they asked if I could assist in the evacuation of the classrooms. The fire department was called immediately and we started the evacuation process. It was quickly determined by the fire department that there was no gas leak. The construction workers from a nearby road hit a gas pipe that released the marker smell, which was mixed with natural gas, into the air, but the natural gas was turned off. Our school ventilation system brought the marker smell into the campus. Since I provided my availability to my administrators, I was able to learn how to evacuate a building successfully, work with the fire department, and execute the campus emergency plan. As aspiring leaders, it's extremely important to be available to assist in any way possible at any time.

Balance Your Time

I went to the front office before school, during my off period, my lunch break, and after school to see what leadership opportunities I could participate in. I had to be very intentional about my time and how I used it throughout my day. My goal was to maintain a high-quality standard in my classroom but get the leadership experiences needed to grow. Since my mission was to get to the front office as many times a day as possible, often, I got to work earlier or stayed later to get my classroom work completed. Depending on the day and the classroom needs, sometimes I was unable to go to the front office. My principal would remind me, "Don't forget, you're a classroom teacher first." Although this statement made me want to work harder to become an administrator, it was true. It's easy to allow your aspirations to cloud your perspective. My classroom responsibilities needed to be my top priority as I balanced my leadership growth.

GROW IN THE UNCOMFORTABLE

When I first began my university's administrative internship, I was provided the opportunity to substitute for three weeks as a Dean of Students at my home campus. The Dean of Students role was primarily to handle the student discipline for the campus. One of our administrators retired mid-year, leaving a position vacant on campus for the remainder of the school year, so the principal selected three teachers to rotate through the role of Dean of Students to gain additional experience. During this time, I was provided an opportunity to learn on the job and grow through very uncomfortable situations.

One afternoon, we had a student who was very upset and frustrated. This student had a history of difficulty with making friends and their emotions escalated quickly. We got a call on the radio that the student was missing from class. My assistant principal and I went to go find the student. We looked down the halls, in the locker room, and in the bathrooms. Suddenly another student came to us and told us there was a student in the 8th-grade bathrooms who appeared to be ill. We both looked at each other and began to rush to the bathroom. My assistant principal jumped up to look over the stall and a shocked look came across the student's face. The missing student was engaging in a self-harming activity in the locked stall. We were able to get the student out, immediately comforted the student, took the student to the nurse, called the school counselor to meet us there, and called the student's parents. The parents came to the school immediately and the conversations were extremely emotional about the steps that were needed to proceed for the student's safety and emotional health. Although I did not participate in the conversation with the parents, I did observe the steps needed to support this student and the parents during an emergency situation and beyond. As a classroom teacher, I never had to speak to parents at such an intense and important level. Before this event, my interactions with parents required a phone call home about a student's minor behavior. This situation gave me a perspective on administration that I didn't know existed.

A year ago, I received a text message from my former assistant principal, and to my delight, it was a picture of her with this student smiling in a store parking lot. The student is now in college and doing fantastic. It was incredible to see this student be successful after so much heartache. As an educator, it is hard to know the impact we make on our students. The end product is much further than we get to see and we have to trust that we are instilling the necessary traits for them to be successful adults.

Although the leadership experiences may be chaotic, emotionally draining, or unpredictable, we all must step out of fear and challenge ourselves in the uncomfortable. We are in a relationship profession, and relationships are difficult. If you aspire to lead, you need to insert yourself in the difficult moments, which may include having a parent cuss at you, a student getting aggressive, or a staff member crying asking for help. You will need to be the calming presence and the guiding voice. However, this will only happen if you get out of your comfort zone to find opportunities to assist and learn.

GO BEYOND YOUR POSITION

At the end of the school year, our Dean of Students took an administrative position in another state, which meant we now had two administrative positions open. Although I was tempted to apply for the Dean position, I knew it was too early in my leadership journey. Over the summer, there was a lot of uncertainty and speculation over who would fill the positions. As a coach, I had summer camps and football practices to attend. One summer day, I was on campus and saw my old Dean of Students in the hallway walking with someone. As I approached, my Dean of Students yelled, "Hey, you need to meet this guy!" He continued to talk about how I was going through the Master's program and how I enjoyed getting administrative experiences. The Dean explained that this was the new assistant principal and she was moving her things into the office. She shook my hand and said, "My name is Sonja Pegram and you are always welcome to come to the front office to get experience. I have an open-door policy." Little did I know, this person would have the most influence and impact on my leadership journey.

At the beginning of that school year, I immediately went to Sonja's office and asked if I could help in any way possible. She was surprised that I took her up on her offer and that I came down during my off period. I don't think she realized what she offered at the time. I was hungry to learn, improve my leadership skills, and get as many leadership experiences as possible. Sonja was right, though. Her door was always open and she allowed me to be a part of many administrative experiences.

As I was pursuing growth as a campus leader, it was apparent that I had competition from other teachers in the building. Four other teachers had completed their principal certification and each felt they were ready to move into an administrative role immediately. It was obvious that if I wanted to advance, I was going to have to show my campus and my district that I had innovative ways to impact well beyond my art classroom. Here are a few ways I set myself apart from the competition and proved that an art teacher could grow into an administrator:

Seek Leadership Positions

After half a semester of my Master's program and being a substitute as the Dean of Students, I realized I did not have a leadership title attached to my position. The first thing I did was begin a conversation about a potential leadership position with my principal. We discussed several possibilities and she decided that I would be a wonderful fit as the Fine Arts Team Leader for the campus. This role allowed me to be the middleman between the elective courses and administration. I knew this was an important step to build my leadership experience, impact my campus in a new way, and show the district that I could lead beyond my classroom.

Solve Campus Problems

I knew I needed to make an impact beyond my classroom, but I didn't know where to look to determine the needs of the campus. In search of identifying potential areas of growth for the school, I asked my administration team for the campus data. I wasn't well versed in deciphering the datasheets, but I tried to immerse myself in the information. After looking through the data, it was obvious which students needed additional support. I did some research on the students identified to investigate the reasons behind their' poor grades. The main reason for the poor grades was that students were not completing their homework. I went to my assistant principal, Sonja, and asked her if I could build a peer-to-peer tutoring program to help support the students who were identified. We sat down and she began to walk through coaching questions to help me determine the logistics of the program, which included funding, resources, location, time, and staffing. I reached out to a neighboring high school to create a tutoring partnership and I submitted two grants to fund the program. Within two weeks, I had the program running with high school students tutoring our 8th-grade students, a couple of teachers to assist, and breakfast for the students.

Community Connection

In addition to the peer-to-peer tutoring program, I saw that some of the identified students were having a difficult time with their decision-making and behavior choices. I created a second program, in collaboration with the first program, to help support the same identified students. The program was a mentorship program and I used our Parent Teacher Association (PTA) members as our mentors. This program was a wonderful way for me to meet the community and talk with parents I had never met before. I conferenced with the principal and the PTA president to lay out the expectations, norms, permission forms, and logistics of the program. We advertised the opportunity through the PTA and one day after school, I held an informational meeting. Based on the information I gathered from the parents, I was able to match students with a mentor. Not all students in the peer-to-peer tutoring group participated in the mentorship program, but the students who did participate in both programs saw a substantial increase in their grades. Based on the data, it was evident that the students who participated in both programs saw a greater gain of success due to their academic and social-emotional needs being met with the mentors and peer tutors.

——

Six Pillars to Empower Leadership
By Evan Robb

When principals encourage teachers to "become more," they change the traditional concept of a teacher. For this to occur, teachers need to be encouraged, empowered, and offered opportunities to lead. In my book, *The Ten-Minute Principal,* I urge principals to free up time to focus on leadership—and share a construct to help administrators and teachers increase their leadership capacity:

"The Six Pillars of Leadership" form the foundation needed to develop creative and innovative school cultures. Whether you're a principal or teacher, it's helpful to reflect on each pillar and how you might integrate them into every aspect of school life.

The First Pillar: Vision

Taking time to discuss the future can inspire principals and teachers to work diligently for positive changes. Discussions of the future help shape priorities— where leaders put their time, what they value, and how they communicate those values! The key to creating a vision is that it must be collective and not a top-down decision. A personal vision is where the leader may want to go; a collective vision is where leaders and the group want to go.

The Second Pillar: Relationships

Effective principals and teachers have the skills needed to establish positive relationships. No formula exists for creating positive relationships. However, there are some common elements that effective relationship builders have: they care, communicate, build trust, develop empathy, and have a sincere interest in others.

There is much truth in this old saying: *students won't care what we know until they know we care.* Leadership doesn't work without establishing relationships.

The Third Pillar: Trust

Just like relationships, building and extending trust must be a daily practice for principals and teachers. Trust can take a long time to be established and it is the building block for positive relationships. Effective principals and teachers foster trusting relationships by making collaborative decisions that can lead to embracing creative thinking and innovation.

Trust and safety always walk hand in hand. The result can be staff, teachers, and students who are more willing to take intentional risks to improve and grow or to let go of what's holding them back.

The Fourth Pillar: Efficacy

A belief that leaders can make a significant difference for a child separates the intentions and motivations between poor and exceptional teachers and administrators. To spread efficacy among a school community and foster collective efficacy, the first three pillars must be firmly in place.

Collective efficacy leads to a school culture that values ongoing learning, collaboration, as well as a congruence among words, actions, and beliefs. The more teaching, learning, communication, and collaborative skills school members have, the stronger personal and collective efficacy becomes.

The Fifth Pillar: A Student-Centered Environment

One program or method of teaching cannot meet the needs of all students. In a student-centered environment, teachers and administrators recognize and accept these differences and make decisions that are in the best interests of all students.

To develop a student-centered approach to learning, teachers need the flexibility to refine and adjust learning experiences so every student improves and grows. For this approach to flourish, ongoing building-level professional learning becomes an important part of a school's culture.

The Sixth Pillar: Instructional Knowledge

Staying current and being a learner, an educator committed to growth and increasing his or her knowledge base enhances the profession and benefits students. Instructional knowledge impacts each of the pillars. Lack of instructional knowledge will inhibit directly or indirectly collaborating to build a vision, relationships, trust, and efficacy, or creating a student-centered school.

When educators embrace a personal and professional responsibility to be learners, they develop the knowledge to grow and, in turn, can help staff and students learn. The choice to continually learn and grow rests with individuals, but the principal can inspire staff by becoming a self-motivated learner and sharing his or her enthusiasm and knowledge.

The Six Pillars: Leadership Guideposts

The pillars work in concert to form a solid and lasting foundation for principal and teacher leadership. They are guideposts and enable you to develop a positive school culture that values learning, teaching, taking risks, showing kindness, building relationships, raising questions, collaborating, and communicating.

Evan Robb, Principal, TEDx speaker, and author Evan Robb is presently principal of Johnson-Williams Middle School in Berryville, Virginia.

———

CALL TO ACTION:

- ASPIRE isn't about a book, a podcast, or a mindset —it is a call to action. If you want to advance in your leadership journey, you can not sit back and wait for opportunities to fall at your feet. As a campus leader, I often hear staff members say they want to become a leader without taking steps to enhance their leadership capacity. It is imperative that you are active in your search for opportunities, create solutions for problems outside of your classroom, and strive to rise to the next level.
- Use the discussion questions below to determine your next steps to start your journey and activate your impact in your organization.

QUESTIONS FOR DISCUSSION

- **What door should you be knocking on to ask for more leadership opportunities?**
- **In the assessment of your campus, how are you able to make an immediate impact on your school?**
- **What projects can you oversee to help your students and build a connection to your community?**

Aspire Podcast Resource

The Ten Minute Principal:
Featuring Evan Robb

2

ASPIRE TO FIND SUPPORT

"The delicate balance of mentoring someone is not creating them in your own image, but giving them the opportunity to create themselves."

— *STEVEN SPIELBERG*

MENTORSHIP IS THE KEY

*I*f there is one aspect of my leadership journey that propelled me to the next level, it was the support I received from my mentors. Finding a mentor—on your campus, in your district, or another part of the world—is vital for the development of any leader. With the guidance of a mentor, an aspiring leader can gain perspective, collaborate, problem-solve, obtain wisdom, and conduct unique leadership tasks.

Throughout my leadership journey, I have sought out and met with many leaders to learn from their experiences and to gain a better understanding of how to improve my skills. Each person had qualities I wanted to embrace and emulate. Before you choose a mentor, you will need to identify leaders who possess the qualities that you wish to follow. In my journey, I encountered four models of mentors who each had a unique influence on my leadership pathway.

The Veteran Mentor

As the title states, the veteran mentor has a vast amount of experience in the field of study and leadership. They possess knowledge and wisdom, but most of all, they are willing to teach you every aspect of the role. My first mentor was my first principal. She had been an educator for 30 years and had a very confident demeanor. After I decided I was going to go back to school to pursue an administration degree, I scheduled a meeting with my principal to discuss my future as a leader. Even though at the time, I had been a teacher at the campus for three years, I didn't know my principal well. I had assumed that to be a good teacher, you needed to do your job well and stay under the radar as much as possible. When we met, I was nervous. I stumbled over my words and I desperately tried to explain that I wanted to build my leadership experience.

I finally stopped mid-sentence and said, "I'm sorry. I'm really nervous. I've always been intimidated by you and your position."

She tilted her head in shock and said, "I never thought of myself as an intimidating person. Well, we need to change that."

By admitting my feelings, the ice was broken in our conversation and I learned that she was a kind, wise, and compassionate leader. Her philosophy of being a principal was that she did not want to micromanage her staff. She hired them to do a job and she trusted each of her staff members to do their job to the best of their ability. If you didn't do your job, she would make sure you were accountable for your actions. As my mentor, she allowed me to be a part of almost every administrative task, meeting, and experience possible. She was extremely inclusive and allowed me to learn firsthand. I am forever grateful for her willingness to teach and provide me with amazing leadership opportunities.

The Rising Star

In the last chapter, I talked about my most impactful mentor, Sonja Pegram, and how she was the most influential person in my leadership story. Sonja, the rising star mentor, rose from teacher to principal in a very large district in two-and-a half years. She ascended through the ranks because she was extremely fearless, passionate, and creative. When I was a teacher and she was the assistant principal, I knew very quickly that there was something very special about her and she was not going to be on our campus for long. It was evident that Sonja was ready to be a principal soon. I made it my goal to have her as my mentor and learn everything I could before she was promoted to another campus.

Thankfully, Sonja had an "open-door policy" and she always allowed any aspiring leader to conference, shadow, or partner with her on administrative projects. As a leader, her goal was to grow more leaders. Once I realized Sonja truly desired to build leadership skills in other people, I made it a point to be in her office every day. I was hungry to learn and didn't want to miss out on the opportunity to learn from her.

As a mentor, Sonja had a gift for teaching through experience. We would talk through leadership philosophies, but it was always followed with a leadership task. She believed that you couldn't truly understand how to lead unless you experienced it. For example, we were talking about discipline and as we were talking, a coach came to the office with a student. The student explained that he was upset with another student and grabbed the other student by the neck, which led to him placing the other student in a headlock. We excused the student from the office and I asked Sonja what she would do for consequences.

She looked at me and said, "You talked with the student. I think you should take this one."

I had handled student discipline before on the campus, so I was confident that I could knock this infraction out quickly. I called the mother of the student on speakerphone to let her know what occurred in gym class and that her son would be assigned in-school suspension for the infraction. What I thought was going to be a simple call turned out to be the opposite. The mother did not agree with the consequences and provided her argument in a very loud and angry tone. The mother of the student said she would be up at the school soon to discuss the matter further. I turned around to see Sonja smiling.

Sonja asked, "What are you going to say to the mom when she gets here?"

It was obvious that Sonja was using this as a teaching moment on parent communication. We discussed my delivery on the phone and the possible perspective of the parent. Soon, the mother was in the front office waiting to speak to me. After Sonja and I introduced ourselves, Sonja had me sit at her desk as she stood to the side. I used the teaching from Sonja to try a different approach and to connect with the mother. Although we were not in agreement with everything, the meeting went much better than the phone call.

After each leadership experience, Sonja would provide feedback. She possesses a gift of providing constructive criticism without crushing your soul, which is critical as a mentor. When I made mistakes, she was honest with me about what I did incorrectly or how it could have been improved. Sonja didn't have all the answers either. As a new leader herself, there were many times we were figuring things out together. If she didn't know something, instead of pretending to know the answer, she admitted her lack of knowledge and we would find the answer together. My development and growth as a leader are due to her tutelage and the many leadership experiences she provided.

The Distant Guide

The distant guide is someone who is helpful from afar and provides wisdom and information through phone conversations, meetings, emails, social media, or video conferencing. The benefit of having a distant mentor is you gain a unique perspective from someone who is outside of your current environment.

Before I was connected on social media, I would travel to meet with principals in the area to discuss their leadership journey and to ask them questions on how to advance my career. Due to the distance, I was only able to conduct these meetings once or twice a year. When my veteran mentor retired, I was nervous about the chance of being promoted in my district. I set up a meeting with a principal in a neighboring district to get his advice on my next decisions.

After he listened to my entire story, the distant guide asked, "You were able to do all of those things as a teacher?"

I laughed and said, "Yes, an art teacher at that."

"Stay where you are. You are getting more opportunities than most could dream of."

He was right, but I needed to hear it from outside of my campus and district. Sometimes, we get so used to the environment and norms of our experience that we don't realize there are other ways of conducting business. At the time, I was questioning many things, including if I needed to move to another district. Based on the guidance from this principal, I was able to experience the most important year in my leadership journey.

The Strategic Planner

The strategic planner mentor is someone who has a wonderful perspective on the strategy of leadership. They have a plan, blueprint, or model for how to rise to the next level. As much as we want to think our skill level is the sole proponent of getting us to the next level, having a mentor to collaborate with on the process of seeking promotion is an invaluable commodity.

When my veteran mentor retired, a new principal was hired for the campus. At first, I was afraid I was going to lose every opportunity I was provided by my previous mentor. As a teacher, I was granted access to meetings and planning sessions that only a few in the building were awarded. Thankfully, my new principal saw value in my leadership skills and believed I could become an administrator the following school year. Due to this belief, the strategic planner developed a plan of action with me to expand my leadership experiences beyond the campus level.

From the first time I met the strategic planner, it was obvious that the person was knowledgeable, crafty, and extremely self-confident in their skills. After one meeting, I realized the guidance from this person was going to be exactly what I needed to become an administrator.

Each one of these mentors was vital to the development of my skills.

During meetings and ongoing conversations with each of these people, I was able to find support through coaching, direction, opportunity, and guidance.

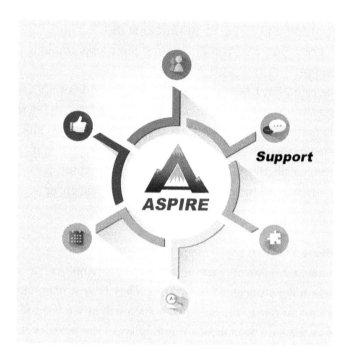

COACHING

At the beginning of my senior year of high school, I had an extremely poor and disappointing soccer tryout. When the tryouts concluded, the varsity coach pulled me aside to say that I didn't make the varsity team. He explained that I had two options:

1. Play Junior Varsity (JV) my senior year
2. Quit playing soccer

I was devastated by the coach's decision and my first reaction was to quit the sport altogether. As I walked back to the campus, the JV coach ran up to me, wrapped his arm around me, and told me how excited he was to have me on his team. At first, I was skeptical but the JV coach quickly shared his philosophy of soccer, my role on the team, and a plan to improve my skills on both sides of the field. Although I was crushed by not making the top team, the JV coach instantly infused hope and excitement into my outlook on the situation. After two games on the JV team, I was promoted to the varsity team. Once I was promoted, I did not get much playing time on varsity, and there were many games I never entered to play. At the end of the season, on "senior night," the coach played all of the seniors for the last 5 minutes of the game. I was playing forward and in the last minute of play, I scored my first and only varsity goal. Of course, I was extremely excited during the game, but I was even more excited to see my JV coach after the game. He yelled with excitement and ran over and gave me a huge hug. He said how proud he was of me and how my hard work paid off. My coach made a giant scene with his excitement and I reveled in every second of it.

As an aspiring leader, we need to find the coach who is going to guide us in the tough times and celebrate our victories. When obtaining a mentor, it's important to find someone who recognizes your strengths, improves your skills, and motivates you to be your best. The coaching model was foundational to my life in athletics and has continued to be the most effective process to enhance my skills as a leader. My mentors, similar to an athletic coach, constantly challenged my abilities, allowed learning through mistakes, and provided honest feedback. We need to be exposed to and practice new leadership experiences. Without a mentor who coaches, we will be lost to our own lack of knowledge, skills, and understanding.

DIRECTION IN UNCERTAINTY

During my junior year of college, one of my college professors pulled me into his office and asked me a very powerful question. The professor was a man of few words with an impactful and stoic presence. Imagine sitting in front of a visual blend of Albert Einstein and Andre the Giant. At this time in his class, I wasn't providing my best effort and was behind on several projects.

The professor asked simply, "What do you love?"

It was an unexpected question since I assumed I was going to be reprimanded for my lack of effort. I didn't know how to answer. The professor saw my confusion and asked me to fold a piece of paper in half. I complied and he told me to create a list in two categories, 'things I love' and 'things that make me happy.' He quickly explained the things that we love we need to hold onto forever. The things that make us happy will not last since they can change with each day. After the meeting, I went home and I made the list, which became my compass going forward.

Through the practice of inquiry, a mentor can provide direction through self-reflection. Using a series of questions and a basic activity, my professor was able to focus and direct my thinking in a positive trajectory. After our meeting, my circumstances didn't change but my outlook changed drastically.

Mentorship is a process to present possibilities and abilities, not dictate beliefs, instill guilt, or demand the decisions of others. It is important to find a mentor who can ask the right questions to challenge our thought process, especially when we feel lost. As a new leader who is experiencing new leadership tasks, it is common to constantly wonder if you made the correct decision.

> "A mentor empowers a person to see a possible future, and believe it can be obtained."
> ~ Shawn Hitchcock

NEW OPPORTUNITIES

As I stated in the last chapter, we must activate our journey and become the "office rat" to seek opportunity. Similarly, obtaining a mentor is another methodology that leads to new opportunities. As we make connections with leaders in the industry that we admire, want to emulate, or believe would propel us to growth, we will increase our knowledge and experience new challenges, tasks, and operations. As you are meeting with your mentor(s), try to find new opportunities in these areas:

Shadow the Position You Seek

When my former principal and mentor provided an invitation to shadow the administrative position and gain additional experience, I took full advantage of the invitation. I was provided a new view of administration with collaborative sessions to solve campus problems, complete tasks, and plan new initiatives. Due to the opportunities offered, I was able to learn the many nuances of the position to prepare myself for future leadership roles. If you aren't able to shadow someone on your campus, reach out to someone on another campus to see if they would be willing to provide you the opportunity.

Participate in New Tasks

To gain additional classroom assessment experience, I asked my principal if I could be trained in our "quick walkthrough" process. The walkthrough system allowed a staff member to enter a class for 3-5 minutes and record the data in an application on your phone. My principal agreed and sent me to the district training on how to run the application and assess the level of student engagement. After my training, I made it my goal to get into as many classrooms as possible to gather data and to observe other amazing teachers. The experience was incredibly valuable. I was able to not only help my campus administrators and district to gather data but also learn many helpful classroom strategies. By participating in the "quick walkthroughs," I was able to show the district that I took the initiative to expand my knowledge while also becoming well-versed in new-to-me educational and classroom management strategies.

Volunteer to Serve

When I began my Master's program, I didn't have any leadership titles and, outside of coaching, I didn't formally participate in any other school functions, clubs, or programs. As I continued to speak to my administrative team about their leadership journeys, I realized I didn't have much experience outside of my classroom. Over the next few years, as committee sponsors, leadership positions, and other opportunities became available, I was the first to volunteer my services. My goal was to learn as much about the inner workings of the campus as possible. Before I knew it, I had volunteered my time by sponsoring a student club, serving on campus committees, leading current campus organizations, serving on district committees, and creating new programs.

GUIDANCE

The longer you are in the role of administration, the more often you realize you need additional guidance. By connecting with other leaders for coffee, lunch, or a formal meeting, I have been able to hear many stories of triumphs and mistakes. Less formal and time-consuming than mentorship, through guidance meetings I have been able to gain wisdom and advice for future actions.

Before each guidance meeting, I created a list of topics or questions I wanted to discuss with other leaders. My goal was to be conscious of their time and be efficient with my questions. It's important that you have a reflective process in place to identify the areas that you need to improve on. For example, as an art teacher, I knew that I needed to learn about instructional design to support the needs of teachers in other content areas. It was by far the most difficult area to gain experience. It required the assistance of other teachers and the administration. Knowing this was an area I needed to improve on, I used guidance meetings with other leaders to gain additional information on instructional practices, curriculum, and assessments.

Receiving advice can be either a risky or rewarding endeavor based on the source of the counsel. It's extremely important to create a support system to provide trustworthy guidance. If we aren't careful, we can construct a circle of deception to feed into our desires, affirming our weaknesses as strengths or feeding our ego. Early in my career, I had a leader who I thought had my best interest in mind and intended to build my leadership skills. Unfortunately, it became obvious that this was far from the case. The leadership opportunities I thought I was being provided were just additional low-level tasks to ease the burden of their job. After that experience, I made sure to guard myself and get to know the person before I asked for leadership guidance. Often, especially early in the journey, we are so hungry to improve, we lose perspective and allow opportunities for deception.

My high school soccer coach used to say, "show me your five best friends and I will show you your future." The same applies to guidance. You have to surround yourself with leaders who have the same values, beliefs, and passions as you. If they don't possess the same core values, your perspective will become warped and your skills can regress.

PAY IT FORWARD

Within the mentorship process, it's imperative to provide others with opportunities to experience new and challenging opportunities to establish growth. Many aspiring leaders don't have the resources to be mentored and grow through this process. This was extremely prevalent when I created an aspiring leaders program for my previous district. Without much advertisement, we had almost two hundred participants who were seeking any chance to learn about leadership. After the event, I had a lot of attendees reach out and let me know that they wished they had a similar program to participate in regularly at their campus or at the district level.

Now, as an administrator, I try to provide the same opportunities to teachers both on my campus and within the district so they can see beyond their classroom. The mentorship process goes beyond conversations. If a teacher is not able to shadow their administrators or they want a different experience on another campus, I always allow aspiring leaders to shadow me. As leaders, we must develop aspiring leaders through active participation in expanded roles and responsibilities. Leaders are not born with all of the skills. They are created through coaching, direction, opportunity, and guidance.

———

Mentorship is a Crucial Role
By Sonja Pegram

 "When I was young, I never wanted to leave the court until I got things exactly correct. My dream was to become a pro. I don't know if I practiced more than anybody, but I sure practiced enough. I still wonder if somebody-- somewhere--was practicing more than me."

— LARRY BIRD

The mentor has a crucial role in helping the world of public education find authentic leaders. The public school system is currently full of what I call "safe leaders." These people are more like managers who complete tasks that have been predetermined and passed down from on high. The safe leader makes sure that all the boxes are checked and then passes the list down to the assistant administrators, who dutifully check the boxes and then pass the list down to the department heads, and so on down to the teachers and students. It's *Groundhog Day.* Authentic leaders are not content with checkboxes. They recognize that campuses, classrooms, and individual students are unique and that solutions to problems require personal involvement and creativity. No two days are the same.

Leadership in public education is bounded by ceilings and walls, and the safe leaders operate within these confines. Compromises are made for all sorts of reasons that have nothing to do with improving conditions for students. We lose so much potential leadership talent because so many people with vision are not willing to be trapped within those walls. Safe leaders, however, operate comfortably behind the walls because they don't want to be seen. They are happy to put the paperwork first and the people second. Paperwork gives them an excuse to hide from the messy business of dealing with real human beings face to face. As a result, I keep my eye out for the special educators who are willing to hustle for greatness, to scavenge for treasure, to battle against unfairness, to turn the walls and ceiling of their rooms to glass. I consider it part of my job to make sure that they know their commitment makes a difference, that we need their unique style of authentic leadership more than ever.

Great educational leaders, like all successful people, start with a burning desire to achieve that which cannot be taught. I believe that the mentor's job is to recognize that drive and become a resource—the voice of experience, a sounding board who can offer suggestions or ask the hard questions about things that we don't want to see or accept. They can embolden us, and, when we need a shove, even push us off the diving board.
Mentors come to us in many forms. Some of us can point to a particular administrator, department head, or fellow teacher that had a singular impact on our development as professionals. But it was not like that for me.

It sounds like a cliché to say that my first mentors were my parents, but the lessons they taught me, often by example, have been the foundation upon which I have erected my career as an administrator. My father grew up poor in Civil Rights-era South Dallas and was a veteran of the Vietnam War. For him, courage was nonnegotiable. He knew that if I backed away from the neighborhood bully as a child that I would become the kind of adult who would shy away from conflict, even if it meant tolerating injustice. My mother was on her own as a parent and often had to struggle financially. Nonetheless, she showed me how to be an independent woman, how not to compromise on anything that might threaten her autonomy. Neither of my parents were professional educators, but I often think about how their mentorship has impacted my approach to the way I try to conduct myself as an educational leader.

A mentor is not someone that we necessarily seek out, and it may not be someone who actively intends to teach us. It might be a captivating spirit—one that takes us by surprise. Someone who arrests us by their mere presence and makes us think, "Woah! What is this about?" Meetings with such people are often a happy accident. They are the sorts of people we stumble over who shock our system. They speak with words that we desire to emulate until we make them our own. When I come across someone like this, I try to identify and analyze the aspects of him or her that I admire. Such people may or may not be fellow educators. During a time of difficult transition in my life, I was befriended by someone who helped me recognize things about myself and my evolving place in the world that has had lasting ramifications for me both personally and professionally. Again, this was not someone that I consciously sought out, but my soul and spirit were on autopilot, and they recognized that in this other person I would not only find support but guidance. Another unexpected and transforming interaction came when a new teacher joined our department and immediately altered the physical environment of his classroom in ways which we hadn't realized were even allowable—he changed the color of the walls, used only indirect sources of light, and brought in area rugs, framed artwork, and real furniture. He challenged our preconceptions about what an inspiring learning environment could look like and how a classroom could feel like a place of privilege. Here was someone who was implicitly saying that we don't have to do things the way they have always been done and that a positive tone can be established before the first word is spoken. I try to make it a habit to apply whatever it is that these influential people have to offer to all areas of my life, not just in the school building. To this day, I devote thought to the way my office is decorated. It has to inspire and delight all members of my learning community. It's a running joke in American culture that we all dread being called down to the principal's office, but I want my principal's office to be a place that everyone is drawn to visit.

I was fortunate to rise through the administrative ranks quickly, so my tenure at any one school was never very long. Perhaps for this reason, I can't point to a particular person who took me under his or her wing. I would have liked to have worked under the direct tutelage of a great leader because I know that there is so much that I could have learned, so many times when I would not have had to improvise. There is no doubt in my mind that the voice of experience can be invaluable to people who are on their way up. But I'm also a firm believer that the mentee has to take it upon him or herself to seek guidance. The desire to become a leader has to be authentic and passionate. For me, leadership is a calling, not a job description; a mission, not a vocation.

I don't seek out protégés, but I will leave a trail of breadcrumbs to my office door. I'll even keep my door open and send out the clearest of invitations, but usually, I don't have to be so overt. In my experience, the people who genuinely seek mentorship are "office rats". The folks who are hungry for knowledge will pursue and devour it. My role is to ensure that the mentees have the opportunity to experience and explore every possible situation, to peer into the darkest of corners. The dedicated will take advantage of every opportunity. Josh Stamper took advantage of being a fly on the wall. In fact, he became a fly in the soup, and he got fed.

I like to sit people down and explain how I see leadership. Education classes don't always teach the dirty truth. I try to be transparent. Do you want to be a great leader? Are you prepared to sacrifice family time? Is your personal life more important to you? What are the regrets that you're prepared to have? If our attitude is going to be "people first, paper second," then the paperwork will have to be pushed back to after hours. The workday is extended; the weekend is shortened. If students are at the core of everything we do and we are genuinely dedicated to putting them first, then it's not realistic to think that our personal relationships won't suffer.

The most important question that a mentor can force you to answer is whether you have the fire to do this. You will be expected to live in track housing. There may be the illusion of difference—laminate as opposed to carpet—but the floor plan is the same. We need you to find a way to build custom houses with hardwood floors in a one-size-fits-all world.

It's fine if people don't really want to commit themselves to educational leadership, but I don't want to overwork myself trying to make someone without the fire into something that he or she does not want to become. But I cannot help but wonder how much talent we are losing because we fail to nurture it. Each year more than 130,000 teachers leave the field for reasons other than retirement. Only twenty percent cite unsatisfactory compensation as their reason for leaving. How many potential authentic leaders might have stayed if they had found the right mentor?

Sonja Pegram, Principal, Guenn Center, Plano, Texas

———

CALL TO ACTION:

No matter where you are in your leadership journey, we all need a mentor. Reflect on the leaders in your life that made the largest positive impact and do the following:

- Create a list of the qualities they possessed and why those qualities impacted you the most.
- Based on the qualities you listed, what leaders do you currently know who possess the same qualities?
- Reach out to the leaders on the list, set up a meeting, and discover your veteran, rising star, distant guide, or strategic planner to assist you in your leadership journey.
- During these meetings and conversations, find support and areas of need through coaching, direction, opportunity, and guidance.

QUESTIONS FOR DISCUSSION

- **Who is your mentor and what qualities would you like to emulate?**
- **As you reflect, what leadership skills do you want to gain or improve?**
- **What opportunities would you like to experience and who can you ask to obtain those leadership opportunities?**

Aspire Podcast Resource

Mentorship is a Crucial Role: Featuring Sonja Pegram

3

ASPIRE TO PERSEVERE

"The difference between a successful person and others is not a lack of strength, not a lack of knowledge, but rather a lack in will."

— *VINCE LOMBARDI*

TAKING THE CHALLENGE

*A*fter I received my Master's in Educational Administration, I was confident that I could be successful at the next level. I applied with the necessary documentation to my district to become an administrator. Several weeks later, I was notified that I was selected to interview in front of a panel of principals. Prior to the interview, I sat down with my campus administrators and conducted a mock interview to work through my thoughts and refine my talking points. It was a valuable experience as I was able to practice and receive immediate feedback from my mentors, which was needed. Most of my initial responses were unstructured and didn't hit at the heart of the questions. Having an opportunity to practice my interview skills and gain advice in a safe space increased my confidence for the first interview.

On the day of my interview, the conference room was intimidating, with five principals seated at a large rectangle table. Although I was nervous, I was confident in my preparation and previous leadership experiences. It wasn't a perfect interview, but based on the non-verbal responses from the panel, I felt my answers resonated with them.

After the interview concluded, a principal walked me to the conference room door. As I was leaving, he whispered, "You did a great job."

I wasn't expecting the compliment but it was wonderful to hear. It was a jolt of confidence and I thought I had a good chance to be placed in the administrative pool. Only a few people a year are selected to the administrative pool. Within a week, I received a call from the district for a second interview. The second interview was the final stage of the interview process with a panel of central office directors.

When I entered the room, I scanned the conference room table. My heart dropped and I began to get extremely nervous as several of the key central office directors were missing from the table. My brain started racing about what their absence implied. My first thought was I needed to be perfect in my responses and perform well for the panel. With each question, I tried to provide the answer I thought they wanted to hear. My nerves transitioned quickly to panic, which was noticeable every time I answered a question. As I was walking out of the district central office, I knew the interview wasn't my best performance. My communication wasn't crisp and I felt I was extremely general in my responses. My only hope for advancement was my principal's recommendation, the impact I made on my campus, and my first interview with the principal panel.

A few weeks later, my wife brought me a letter from the mail. As soon as I saw the school district's logo, I felt ill because I knew the content of the letter would change the trajectory of my professional career. As I opened the envelope, I sat down at the kitchen table. My eyes quickly scanned the letter to see that I was denied entry into the district's administrative pool.

Anger engulfed me. I slammed my fist onto the table and yelled, "What else am I supposed to do? I've done everything on that campus!"

I was beyond disappointed. I was defeated.

FEAR OF FEEDBACK

When I returned to school, I let my principal and assistant principal know that I did not get selected for the administrative pool. It was a difficult conversation with my assistant principal, who spent the entire year mentoring me. I felt like I let myself down, but even more so, I felt like I let her down. Sonja was inspirational in my development as a leader. She tried to lift my spirits, encourage me, and instill hope, but it didn't change my outlook. We reviewed the interview questions and my responses to the panel to determine if I made any errors. As I was breaking down my responses to the interview questions, my principal, the "veteran mentor," interrupted our meeting and asked me if I wanted to get feedback from the Director of Secondary Schools. Embarrassed by my failure, I looked down and suddenly began to feel sick to my stomach. I reluctantly agreed.

We walked into the principal's office and my principal explained that she called the district to gain feedback on my interview. We sat down and my principal continued to explain that the Director of Secondary Schools left a long message on her answering machine, which included the areas the panel thought I needed to grow in.

My principal said, "Before I press play, I don't believe everything that is said in this message to be true. It's going to be hard to listen to but I think you should hear the feedback. Are you sure you want to listen to the message?"

I agreed to listen to the message, and my principal was right. It was extremely hard to hear. The director's message went into great detail, with an exhaustive list of areas I needed to learn before I moved to the next level, such as special education, instructional leadership, campus data, celebrating diversity, and many more topics. I sat there with my head down as each word felt like a gut punch. It was clear I didn't communicate my experience and knowledge clearly to the panel of district leaders. After listening to the message of constructive criticism, I questioned my ability to communicate in an interview and whether I had a future in the field of administration.

PERSEVERANCE REQUIRES HOPE

After receiving the denial letter from the district, my ego took a huge hit. I felt like I was ready to move to the next level, and I was confident that due to my experience on the campus, I was going to be promoted immediately. The tough part of not being promoted in education is, generally, you have to wait another calendar year to begin the interview process again. The idea of working in the same role for another school year and having the entire staff know I failed was hard to stomach. It felt like I had a blinking red sign on my chest that said "Loser." Several teachers voiced to me that they thought I was too young or inexperienced to be an administrator. In my mind, coming back in the same role proved they were right. I had to decide if I was going to give up on my goals, stay at my current campus, or move to another campus or district.

My principal, the veteran mentor, retired at the end of the school year. She allowed me to experience everything an administrator would experience. I was invited to each administrative meeting and training available. The veteran mentor met with me often to provide advice and she advocated for me to become an administrator. That year, I was even granted a long-term sub for my class to serve as the Dean of Students, which allowed me to handle the entire student body's discipline. The amount of experience and guidance I received was invaluable.

When the new principal was announced, I was extremely nervous that he wouldn't want to invest in my development as a leader. Based on the feedback I received, the district had a perception that I was lacking certain leadership skills, and I feared the new principal would have the same belief.

During that summer, I was angry with the feedback I received from the district. I was quick to decide that my current position wasn't going to prepare me for administration. When I reached out to my assistant principal and mentor, we began to discuss the possibility of transferring to another campus to fill the role of the behavior specialist, which is a position specifically working with student behaviors. The campus with the behavior specialist opening had a more diverse population, and the position would provide new leadership experiences. Before I applied, my new principal reached out and asked to meet with me. I didn't want to make any rash decisions, so I agreed to meet with him before I applied for the behavior specialist position.

Before the meeting, I had all of my talking points prepared and evidence available to present my leadership experience. I wanted to prove to him that I was a valuable asset to the campus and I was prepared to be an administrator. As I began talking through the many leadership tasks I had completed, the initiatives I developed and the various campus groups I was associated with, the new principal stopped me.

He asked, "Who, at the district, knows you do all of these things on this campus?"

The questions stopped me dead in my tracks. I didn't have an answer.

He followed up by asking, "What programs have you participated in at the district level?"

I said, "I haven't done anything at the district level."

He smiled and paused before explaining that it was obvious I was an asset to the campus, but the issue was that the district's central office didn't know anything about my leadership skills. The only information they received was secondhand. If I wanted to make an impactful impression, I needed to be visible at the district level, and the district directors needed to be invited to the campus to see firsthand how I was leading on my campus.

This *one* conversation with my new principal changed my perspective completely and provided the most important aspect of perseverance. Hope.

We continued to talk through an action plan of the district programs I was going to participate in, how to increase my knowledge in the areas that I was lacking, and how I was going to communicate my skill to the panel of district directors. For the first time, I felt like I had a clear-cut plan of tangible steps. It was clear that I did not need to transfer to gain the experience necessary to be an administrator.

GETTING OFF THE GROUND

As I stated in the last chapter, mentorship is the key to any leader's success. Although Sonja (The Rising Star) continued to be my mentor, my new principal (The Strategic Planner) became a valued guide too. Sonja prepared me for the day-to-day operations of the campus, and my new principal steered me through the political aspect of the administrative process. I met with both of them regularly and our conversations expanded to new topics relating to administration.

My new principal continued to hammer home an idea that I heard often as a child. Growing up, my dad would always say, "It's not what you know; it's who you know." Throughout my life, the saying irritated me because it seemed disingenuous. *Why would anyone be successful and get what they wanted just because they knew someone? What if they didn't deserve it?* Although I disliked the saying and what it stood for, as I grew older, I found truth in these words. I knew I had to dust myself off, get out of my comfort zone, and make connections at the district level to advance.

BREAKING THE COMFORT ZONE

Although I initially thought another year in the same role was going to be useless, it turned out to be the year I broke out of my introverted shell and began to embrace being uncomfortable at a different level. Often, our comfort in our current situation limits our growth to small increments. This is a disservice to ourselves and the people we serve. We have to fight through fear, safety, and failure to enhance our skills. It was evident that I failed in several areas of the process to advance in my district. The failure was not going to define me as a leader. I was determined to prove everyone wrong and, through the guidance of my principal, I constructed an action plan to set out beyond my campus and my comfort zone for the upcoming school year. The steps were the following:

1. Participate in a district committee
2. Make connections with district leaders
3. Obtain grants for my campus programs
4. Present at campus staff meetings
5. Invite district directors to a campus initiative

Participate in a District Committee

As the new school year began, the district sent out an email to all the district principals requesting names for the District Based Improvement Committee (DBIC). This committee was made up of district teachers, campus administration, district administration, community members, and parents. As soon as my principal received the email, he brought me in to discuss the opportunity. The strategic planner explained that he was a member of the DBIC when he was a teacher and he felt the opportunity allowed him to get a better understanding of the district, while meeting and collaborating with important leaders across the district. The issue was there were only a few seats open for the committee, and you had to be voted on the committee. The entire district received an email with the names of the candidates and the results of the vote would determine if I was on the committee. This process was not my favorite exercise because I needed to campaign for a seat on the committee. My principal advised me to send an email to the entire campus staff and anyone I knew in the district, requesting they vote for me. Although it made me uncomfortable to ask people for votes, I sent multiple emails to everyone I knew in the district to campaign for votes. A week later, I received an email with a list of members. I quickly scanned the email to see that I was voted onto the district committee and I would be serving on the DBIC for two school years. It was a huge first accomplishment in our newly constructed action plan and provided me with a great deal of confidence to move forward.

Make Connections with District Leaders

In being selected and attending DBIC meetings, I was provided the opportunity to be our campus representative for district board meetings. My role was to take notes at each board meeting and construct an email to our campus staff detailing important district decisions, events, regulations, and policies. If any teachers on our campus wanted a topic or concern to be addressed at the school board meeting, I was nominated to bring the campus' concern to the board when the floor was open. Although the board meetings took additional time in the evenings, I was able to learn valuable aspects of the district and be visible to important district leaders. The topics covered in these meetings were extremely enlightening and each helped me understand the many facets of education, including budgets, social issues, district policies, and procedures.

Obtain Grants for My Campus Programs

One of the dilemmas I had with my mentorship and peer tutoring programs was that I was utilizing campus funds, with my prior principal's approval, for food, supplies, and additional staffing. My new principal, the strategic planner, informed me that he preferred to allocate those funds elsewhere and he wanted my programs to be funded through grants instead. An additional benefit of having the programs funded by grants was that it showed I could fund initiatives by myself without the assistance of a campus budget. We did some research, constructed several proposals, and applied for multiple grants. This was a new experience, so I reached out to several teachers and leaders to gain insight on how to write a grant. My goal was to raise two thousand dollars for my two programs by the beginning of the new school year. Since the grants were not awarded until September or October, my principal provided the funding for the first two months. Within the first month, I had been awarded two grants to achieve my goal of raising two thousand dollars, including one from my district.

Present at Campus Staff Meetings

Before this school year, I had never presented in front of my peers or an adult audience. My principal recommended that I start to share information on a larger scale, and he laid out what professional development topics he wanted to be disseminated to the staff that school year. Based on the topics laid out, we decided on several that I felt comfortable speaking on and we discussed my knowledge of each item. During two staff meetings, I presented on grading practices and creating an online collection of resources. Both presentations were well received and I began to become more comfortable amplifying my voice to other adults.

Invite District Leaders to Campus Initiatives

The last item on the action plan was the one that made me the most uncomfortable. Throughout the school year, our administrative team discussed creative ways to invite the district directors to the campus to see all the wonderful things our students, staff, and community had accomplished. My principal would use these opportunities to highlight my leadership skills and show them I was prepared to be an administrator. It became obvious that my principal was very intent on having the Director of Secondary Schools attend multiple events at our school, and he continued to send invitations throughout the year. Of course, I was nervous because this was the same director who left a long voice message for my previous principal on areas I needed to improve on as a leader.

We planned a celebration of our school's 10th anniversary and invited several district administrators to attend the event. After the festivities were complete, my principal and I walked around the room and thanked every district administrator for attending the event. My principal made a point to talk with the Director of Secondary Schools, highlighting the school year activities and the initiatives I was leading. I was extremely grateful that my mentor felt comfortable to share my accomplishments and fight for my advancement in the district.

At the end of the school year, my principal asked to have the district's middle school principal meeting at our campus. The request was granted and my principal began preparing for the event. We had student greeters at the door to walk every middle school principal, assistant principal, and district administrator to our meeting room. To open the meeting, the Director of Secondary Schools walked to the front of the room, thanked everyone for attending, and thanked our administrative team for hosting the meeting. We were seated in front of the room and I was sitting in the middle of my administrative team.

The director looked at me and said with a grin, "Before we begin, we have a guest at our meeting."

My whole body became stiff. I knew I was the only guest in attendance and, typically, at a principal meeting, any guests would be introduced and the campus principal would say a few words about the aspiring leader. I assumed this procedure would occur again but the director caught me off guard. The director spoke about my positive leadership qualities, how hard I had worked as a leader, and what a valuable asset I would be to a campus administrative team. I was in shock. Just nine months prior, I listened to some extremely difficult feedback, but on this day the perception of my leadership skills was very different.

My principal leaned over and whispered, "I have never seen the director do that. Ever. You're in."

I turned to my assistant principal and she was grinning ear to ear. She wrote on my notepad, THAT WAS AMAZING. Although it was an incredible moment, I knew I had plenty of work ahead of me to get to the next level. My focus quickly turned from my action plan of district involvement to preparing for the interview process of the Administrative Intern pool.

———

Find Your Voice as a Leader
By Latrese Younger

As you ascend into leadership, you lose a much-needed characteristic trait that no one bothers to share with you before your ascension. Unfortunately, you will lose your natural ability to please virtually every adult you encounter in a school building. Most school leaders are former popular teachers—they are often those individuals who are naturally positive, optimistic, and who enjoy solving problems and generating new ideas for their schools. You may have been the go-to person when teachers needed support or the students' choice for the best teacher in the building. When you become a school leader, you are going to lose some of that "likeability." You will sometimes say things that will not sound favorable. You will do things that will cause others to question your judgment and/or competence simply because it does not align with their personal wishes. You will intervene in situations that warrant or demand your intervention and the students, families, and/or staff you serve may not give you a thumbs up, kudos, or a pat on the back for your mandated reporting skills.

With all of the changes that you will undergo as a newly appointed school leader, I need you to brace yourself for what I know to be true. I want you to expect the unexpected and embrace the chaotic messes that will ensue as a result, because they will only make you a more competent, fearless, and resolved leader as you progress in your career. Not only will you be better and stronger as a leader because of all of the things you will encounter as a new leader, but you will also be in a position to do exactly as I am doing one day—preparing the next generation of school leaders to walk and serve in excellence. It is always crucial for aspiring leaders to hear about the pitfalls and hurdles experienced by seasoned administrators. It offers solace and reassures the fact no leadership journey is without hard lessons learned. We would not be very good educators if we did not take time to pause and reflect on our shortcomings and how we can use those experiences to grow and to prepare others for their own journeys.

When I first took the leap from classroom teacher to school leader, I served as a Literacy Director coaching ELA teachers. I always laugh as I share this story because I know that I owe those very patient teachers my most sincere apology. I came into their school like a bull in a china shop—changing and assuming everything and asking nothing. I did not hold what the teachers did each day in high regard or any regard; actually, I only saw the school's present failure as an indication that they were the problem. As you have probably guessed by now, I was not liked at all in that position. I was shunned and avoided. No one was honest with me and no one felt they could trust me to help them grow. I learned very quickly that asserting a posture of "knowing it all" was not my voice; it was a façade, and I needed to "abort, abort, abort"!

By the time I started my next position as a Data and Assessment Analyst in a district central office, I was a markedly different leader. I had had time to think very long and hard about the type of leader I wanted to be. I decided that I wanted to be true to my values and core beliefs. I wanted to exhibit my faith and operate in a way that glorified my Savior. I treated people as humans and not commodities needing repair. I worked tirelessly to develop my listening skills—listening intently before formulating a response. I pulled off the mask that had almost tarnished my leadership career even before it could get off the ground. I made people's growth and personal development my focal point moving forward. I did not worry so much about assigning blame when I was asked to problem-solve, but on the contrary, I thought about how I would feel if I were in each person's shoes. That helped me choose words that healed, uplifted, and encouraged rather than those that belittled or carried condescension.

Now, as a four-year Assistant Principal, I can see the fruits of that labor. Finding my voice has been a long journey, but it has been worthwhile. While I still may not get everything right all the time, and while people may still disagree with my decisions or solutions to problems, no one ever questions my motivation. My core values and beliefs permeate everything I do and say and that leaves little room for ambiguity. As you accept and walk into your new leadership position, I want you to believe in the power of your voice. Make it your main instrument to becoming the leader you are meant to become.

Latrese Younger, Administrator, Educator, and Advocate

———

CALL TO ACTION:

By no means am I promising that my previous action steps will get you the promotion you desire; however, I do believe everyone must have a plan of action to achieve their goals. When creating an action plan, take these questions into account:

- Who at the district can I connect with to learn more about the position I desire?
- What projects or initiatives can I invite other leaders to or to participate in?
- How am I sharing my expertise with others and communicating at a larger scale?
- What district committees or focus groups can I participate in?

As you create your action plan, make sure to gain guidance from a mentor or someone with experience. Without the guidance of a mentor, it will be like traveling in the dark. You may reach your destination but you are going to have a difficult time navigating your surroundings. With a guide, you are more likely to miss the obstacles in your way and get to your destination promptly.

QUESTIONS FOR DISCUSSION

- **Who are you able to speak with to gain authentic and honest feedback?**
- **How can you overcome a previous failure in your leadership journey?**
- **What are some leadership experiences you can participate in that will get you out of your comfort zone?**

Aspire Podcast Resource

*Authenticity is Key:
Featuring Latrese Younger*

4

ASPIRE TO IDENTIFY

> *"Identity cannot be found or fabricated but emerges from within when one has the courage to let go. "*

> — *DOUG COOPER*

DISCOVERING A NEW IDENTITY

 s you grow as a leader in your building or organization, your roles and responsibilities will be enhanced on your campus. With this shift in roles, the relationships and how you are viewed by your colleagues will change too. Many veteran leaders have experienced this, and it may be occurring now in your journey. Regardless, I want to bring this to your attention to help you through the evolution of your leadership identity. In this chapter, we will be identifying what type of leader you want to become and the areas in which you want to grow.

With any new leadership role, as your influence expands, your communication and interactions increase dramatically. Colleagues you rarely spent time with previously are now being impacted by your decisions. It's important to identify how you are perceived by your peers and determine what type of leader you want to be viewed as.

When I began my leadership journey, I had only been in the classroom as a teacher for three years. I didn't interact with many of my peers and I kept to my classroom. During my fourth year of teaching, I became a coach, started my administrative internship, led campus initiatives, participated in multiple committees, and subbed as the Dean of Students. To say that my role changed quickly would be an understatement. I went from a colleague "never seen" to teacher leader "always around." The shift was not smooth as my responsibilities increased dramatically. I noticed a drastic change in how people interacted with me on a personal and professional level.

A part of my Master's program required me to participate in an "Administrative Internship." This allowed me to complete many administrative tasks and get a glimpse of the position. As I began working with the administrative team more, I started to notice a shift in how people perceived and acted around me. In conversations, my colleagues became more guarded and increasingly distant. When I entered a classroom, the teacher became nervous and their body language became stiff, as though I was there to check on their performance. The friends I had on campus began to make comments about me "Going to the Dark Side," being the "Chosen One," or becoming the "Golden Boy" on campus. The first few times it occurred, I laughed it off. But it didn't stop. Moving forward, I tried not to respond and distance myself from those conversations.

As a leader, I tend to get overly focused on my goals and what I need to accomplish. This can be both a strength and a weakness. Early as a leader, I was so determined to have my hands in every aspect of the campus, to learn as much as possible in a short time, I ignored the comments and how people responded to me. What I didn't realize was, with the quick and increased role change, my coworkers didn't agree with the leadership opportunities I was provided. There were many reasons my coworkers didn't accept my new leadership role and they were not afraid to share their opinions. During my first year as an aspiring leader, I heard many statements of doubt, such as:

- Didn't have enough experience in the classroom.
- Didn't possess a leadership role on campus before subbing for the "Dean of Students."
- Just an "art teacher."
- Taking on too many responsibilities to be effective.
- Too young.

Although the comments were annoying, the shift in my new identity didn't hit me until the day I was confronted by my coworker.

THE PERCEPTION OF COMMUNICATION

A few days before a staff meeting, a colleague came to my classroom asking me to review their presentation. They printed the PowerPoint slides and provided me with the packet to look over. I was honored by the request and I wanted to provide impactful feedback.

The layout of the meeting was to meet as a whole staff and then break out into smaller groups. Each session was fifteen minutes and the staff would rotate through each session. We both were asked by the principal to speak to the staff on a different topic for our session. My coworker was nervous about speaking and the quality of the presentation. That evening, I reviewed the presentation and made notes with helpful tips and suggestions on the content of several slides. The next morning, I placed the packet of written feedback in my colleague's box and emailed them that it was completed.

Later in the day, during my off period, the teacher opened my classroom door. I could immediately tell something was wrong.

My co-worker quickly walked to my desk, with the packet in hand, and started yelling, "I don't care if you're a leader on this campus, you are not my boss and you will not tell me what to do! If you become an administrator here one day, that's fine, but you are not one now!"

I tried to respond but all that came out of my mouth was, "Whoa. What?"

Before I could respond any further, the teacher stormed out.

I sat there for a few minutes, racking my brain to remember what I wrote. What feedback did I provide that created such an emotional response? As I thought about my feedback, I became more confused about the response. It was evident that I no longer was viewed as a peer. My feedback and communication had greater weight than I realized. After school, I went to the teacher's classroom and apologized. I tried to explain that my intention was only to help. Unfortunately, the damage was done and our working relationship was never the same.

After reflecting on this experience many years later, I realize that many people aren't actually looking for true feedback. Most are just looking for validation to defeat the doubts they already possess. In this situation, my colleague was nervous about the presentation and was looking for support. Instead of lifting them up, I was more concerned about showing my expertise, which provided criticism and correction.

The job of a leader is to increase motivation, inspiration, and confidence. On this day, I learned the value and weight of my words.

IDENTIFYING LEADERSHIP QUALITIES

It was obvious that I didn't have control of how I was perceived by others on my campus. The harder I tried to hide from the "dark side" or "golden boy" reputation, the louder it became. It was evident that the only control I had was of my actions. My colleagues were having a tough time with my transition from teacher to administrator and I realized I couldn't control their feelings. Instead of focusing on the things I couldn't control, I began to ask, "What leadership qualities do I want to be identified by?" These are the areas I began to focus on and intentionally control.

Energy

My colleagues viewed me as a young teacher with little experience in the classroom and as a leader. I needed to prove I was an asset to them and the campus. It didn't matter the task, I would try to help. Instead of leading with my words, I utilized my time to assist others, which included moving furniture, cleaning, or making copies. Energy is extremely contagious and I wanted to inspire others through my acts of service. My goal each day was to try and help as many people as possible in a short period of time and try to make every interaction with the staff a positive and energized experience.

Positive Attitude

When you are an aspiring leader, you want to say yes to everything and I did just that. I wanted to be the "go-to guy" on campus to show I was a valuable asset. It would have been easy to say no and turn people away. However, I made it my mission to stay positive and help as much as I could each day. The staff didn't need anyone coming onto campus, complaining and hurting the cohesion of the school. If I was unhappy or upset about something, I went to my mentor. I didn't complain to my peers. My goal was to be the light in someone else's day to improve the perception of their situation. As a leader, I wanted to ensure that my attitude was contagious to other people to create a positive trend. Positivity is a powerful tool to enhance communication, relationships, and productivity. Similar to energy, I wanted my colleagues to be led by my positive actions.

Eagerness to Learn

Being new to my leadership role, I wanted to learn every aspect of the school from as many people as possible. Since I was just beginning my leadership experience, I had very little knowledge of the operations of a school. My thinking was, if I knew everything about my campus, I could translate the procedures and processes to my next campus as an administrator. To accomplish this goal, I had to be eager to learn and constantly ask questions. My mentor, Sonja Pegram, continued to push me to ask questions. I would never know the answer unless I asked the question. Most times, I brought a notepad of paper with me to the front office so I could take notes on what I experienced. To gain additional knowledge, I tried to attend every meeting I could and shadowed every leader on campus. Knowledge is power and I wanted to make sure I learned everything before I became an administrator.

BREAKING THE TEACHER IDENTITY

Being an elective teacher is a joy and I loved so many aspects of the position. I knew many of my students came to school for the sole purpose of participating in art or athletics. When I began to show interest in leadership, the reactions I received from many peers were off-putting and followed by questions of doubt. As you can imagine, there are not many art teachers that become administrators in a school.

Even to this day, it's always interesting to witness people's reactions after I've told them that I was an art teacher. The response is a mixture of shock, confusion, and disappointment. In my experience, the perception of what occurs in an art room and what an art teacher does is underwhelming. The course is naturally different from core classes, but many of the teaching strategies and techniques are the same. It was obvious that I needed to change the perception of what I had to offer as an educator. I was not just an art teacher and I was not just a coach. My goal was to prove to everyone that my skill set went well beyond the art room.

In my first interview with the panel of district directors, based on how they asked their instructional leadership questions, it was clear they were concerned about the subject matter I taught and how it could translate into helping other teachers' instruction. I was not confident in my answers and I had to speak on what I would hypothetically do instead of drawing from my past experiences.

To break the stigma of being "just an elective teacher," I conducted over 200 walkthroughs during the school year and logged the data into our district's walkthrough system. I wanted to make it abundantly clear to the district leaders that I had the skills to go into another teacher's classroom, document what occurred, and provide feedback to our teachers.

When I began the walkthrough process, for the most part, I was not greeted with open arms. The teachers were suspicious of my intentions and wanted to know what I was recording. Their fear was that I was taking notes on their performance and reporting back my findings to the administrative team. In fact, that was the opposite of what I was doing. The classroom walkthrough online system allowed me to enter from its drop-down menu only on the students' performance, which included topics of technology use, level of student learning, assessment type, and project categories. I realized quickly that I needed to do these three things each time I entered a classroom:

1. Ask the teacher's permission to conduct a walkthrough, even if it was through nonverbal communication, such as a thumbs-up.
2. Share what data the walkthrough system was recording.
3. Share with the teacher what I recorded after the walkthrough.

In many cases, the teachers did not know me well or were uncertain of why I was observing the classroom. They didn't know if they could trust my intentions or my actions. To break the barrier of mistrust, I tried to show that I had nothing to hide and that I was trying to help everyone involved.

To go a step further, I printed the data from the walkthroughs, which provided pie charts, graphs, and the percentages of how often classroom strategies and resources were being used, and I met with each group of subject teachers to disseminate the data. My administrative staff and I were able to meet with each core subject team and discuss the data to find trends, areas of strength, and areas of improvement.

The classroom walkthroughs were not only beneficial for me as an aspiring administrator, but they also were helpful to me as a teacher. I was able to bring many strategies back to my classroom to improve my own classroom assessments, collaborative groups, and classroom management. When it was time to interview for the Dean of Students position, I would have plenty of experiences to discuss how I was an instructional leader to provide additional support and resources to the teachers.

IDENTITY FRAMEWORK

During the second semester of my sixth year of teaching, I began focusing on the next steps of the process to be promoted to the next level. I met with my assistant principal, and she wanted me to focus on who I was as a leader and reflect on all the things I had accomplished as an aspiring administrator. To work through my ideas, I started to write down characteristics I wanted others to see in me. As I determined who I wanted to be based on my strengths and areas to improve, I created a rough framework to determine my leadership identity. Below is a reconstructed framework of a segment of this process.

Leadership Identity	How would I like to be described and viewed as a leader?
Leadership Goals	What will I accomplish individually, for the campus, and in my district?
Leadership Evidence	What are the outcomes of my initiatives, decisions, and programs?

Leadership Identity

One of the first items I reflected on as a young leader was how I was viewed by my peers. There were several mistakes I had made and relationships that were fractured, which affected the success of certain initiatives. To flush out my ideas, I wrote down the qualities I planned to focus on as a future administrator, including fostering a positive impact on others. I wanted those I served to experience a positive and an effective interaction.

Leadership Goals

We mustn't lose focus on our short- or long-term goals. If we don't write them down, we most likely will lose our focus during the school year. As leaders, we are constantly finding solutions to new problems and assisting in new campus or district initiatives. To remain on task and focused, I had my personal, campus, and district goals visible, so I would see them each day as a reminder to spend some time working toward completing each.

Leadership Evidence

At the end of the school year, I gathered all of my data from my initiatives and made sure I knew the impact my programs made on individual students and the campus. I studied the student data and memorized the increase in student scores to be able to communicate it in a future interview. I needed to prove I was more than a classroom teacher. I needed to show I was able to make my vision a reality and garner results.

———

Finding Your Identity as a Leader
By Sarah Johnson

Our leadership identities can be formed in several ways, some over which we have control over and others based on circumstances beyond our orchestrations. Finding your identity as a leader can take years, developing through challenge and refining through triumph. However, did you know that who you become as a leader does not have to *happen* to you? Though the organizations we serve and circumstances all around us may (will) shift, we can find our leadership identity by intentionally seeking and refining who we are as leaders regardless of what surrounds us. We do that through building our own foundations along the journey by making space to truly understand ourselves as people, setting our purpose, being intentional with our focus, and choosing to lead with our hearts. When we choose to define what each of those pieces means for us, we can lead through those lenses instead of by chance. Unfortunately, so many leaders fall into the trap of trying to become what they feel others want of them—who they think their organization wants or what society expects of them instead of creating the identity of a leader they know they should be, despite what they perceive others want. Or honestly what others outright demand.

Who you are as a leader should not be something that you

stumble upon inadvertently as you navigate the course of any given day. Instead, developing your leadership identity can and should be a deeply intentional journey. What may astonish those of you reading Joshua's book who have not yet experienced the way a leadership title can devour you whole is that you can choose to define your identity in the role—not the role defining you. What a beautiful truth that we are all vastly different and beautifully unique! As a leader, you bring your flavor to the title, not the other way around. If we lose ourselves to our roles, we can suffer from an identity crisis—which will lead us down a path of destruction eventually.

So, how can a person find their leadership identity?

When I work with aspiring administrators in the courses I teach or with the clients I coach who are actively engaged in administrative roles, it is reinforced for me over and over that we do not spend time developing ourselves as leaders enough once we hit the ground running in our titled roles. We go through a program, checking a box to be able to gain a license and eventually take a contract. Maybe when we start, we feel all the study of policy, legal aspects, human resources, culture and climate building, instructional leadership, and all that is required of us prepares us. Until we are hit with tough decisions and leading in real circumstances with real people in the real world and not just in a case study. It is then that we must lean into our foundations.

Friends, I believe with my whole heart that the best way to find your leadership identity is to spend time seeking it intentionally. Spend time understanding your own emotional intelligence capabilities and your abilities to be self-aware and self-regulate. Understand how you gain and use your energy, the way you process information, whether you prefer to plan or to take calculated risks, if you are a visionary or taskmaster—and consider how all of these elements contribute to how you lead. Make space to develop, refine, and define your values so that you can live aligned with them in your leadership. Create a personal leadership mission and vision statement, and lead every day through those lenses. Develop a habit of refining priority and living with intentionality in your calendar, your decision-making, and your service to others, and finally, learn how to cultivate a wholehearted version of yourself so you can lead strong through all challenges. Your leadership identity is inextricably tied to you, friends. As Brene Brown says, "Who we are is how we lead." If we do not make intentional space to truly understand who we are, we will never truly understand how we lead. Don't wait around to find your leadership identity through trial and error. Seek it intentionally, building firm foundations so you can rise up, slay fear, and serve well now and throughout your leadership journey.

Sarah Johnson, Leadership Coach, Podcaster, Author, Speaker, Educator, @Sarah Johnson

———

CALL TO ACTION:

You have the power and the ability to be any type of leader you desire. However, it will not happen overnight. To be an effective leader, you must know your strengths, values, beliefs, goals, and passions. If you don't know who you are as a leader, you will waver in your decisions and convictions, which will cause inconsistencies and confusion in your organization. Take time to identify and write down your goals, mission statement, and leadership qualities. As the year continues, review and focus on the areas you need to work on and the items you have accomplished. This practice will strengthen you as a leader and make you more effective for your organization.

QUESTIONS FOR DISCUSSION
Using the Identify Framework:

- How would I like to be described and viewed as a leader?
- What will I accomplish individually, for the campus, and in my district?
- What are the outcomes of my initiatives, decisions, and programs?

Aspire Podcast Resource

Facing Self Doubt:
Featuring Sarah Johnson

5

ASPIRE TO REFLECT

*"Without **reflection**, we go blindly on our way, creating more unintended consequences, and failing to achieve anything useful. In our daily life, we encounter people who are angry, deceitful, intent only on satisfying their own needs. "*

— *MARGARET J. WHEATLEY*

I BET IT'S NOT OFTEN

I was sitting in a leadership presentation when I heard the speaker state, "How often do you set time aside to reflect on your previous actions and practices as a leader? I bet it's not often." The speaker paused and let the audience contemplate his words. As I looked around the conference room, I thought for a moment and realized, *it's true*. I didn't sit down and spend time reflecting on my previous actions as a young leader. Each day was about moving forward, not looking backward. Why was that? Was I too busy or did I not value the practice? When I was starting to become a leader on my campus, my eyes were only on the future with one goal in mind, which was to become an administrator as soon as possible. As I was sitting there, I decided I needed to change my practices, find an avenue to reflect, and determine how to improve my skills.

CHALLENGED TO REFOCUS

After I got back to campus from the leadership conference, my reflective mindset and practices did not change. I went right back to my routines and continued to have tunnel vision on my goal of becoming an administrator. My eyes were only focused forward on gaining additional leadership experience for my resume.

One day as I was in the front office looking to help the administrative team during my off period, my principal brought me into his office and asked me to sit down. From across his desk, he asked, "What is your position?"

I was confused by the simplicity of the question and I hesitantly answered, "An art teacher."

He smirked and asked, "How are you doing in that position?"

I quickly answered, "Yeah, I'm doing fine. Why?"

"Well, before school, during your conference period, during your lunch break, and after school, you are working with the administrative team. When are you able to be an art teacher?" The comment cut deep because I knew he was right. I was helping in so many administrative tasks and had my hands in so many projects that it was impossible to be a great teacher.

My principal continued, "I understand you want to be an administrator and gain experience but at what expense? You need to be excellent in your current role to be ready for the next level."

The assessment was correct. As a teacher, I was doing just fine. Not excellent. It was obvious that I was letting my classroom responsibilities slide, and as much as my principal appreciated my help, my classroom should always be my top priority.

"I would advise you to take some time to prepare your application, letter of intent, and your interview answers. You probably won't be here next year."

It was at this time that I took a step back from overextending myself. As I spent less time in the front office, I began to prepare myself for the next steps in the application process and truly reflect on my leadership practices. As I was constructing my leadership vision and statements, I began to reflect on the past two years of leadership. When I looked back at my leadership experience, I realized that I had gone through some difficult situations and made many mistakes.

In this chapter, I want to be transparent with my mistakes and share the importance of reflection. With these stories of challenges and failures, I hope you can use them as a guide to navigating around the potential landmines in your leadership journey.

Pitfall #1: Overstepping the Boundary

I was sitting at my desk when I heard, "What the $#%@ are you doing? It's not your turn to be in this position! Whenever it's your turn, that's when you get to make the decisions." When I turned around, I found the acting Dean of Students standing at my desk angrily pointing at me.

I stood up and said, "Dude, what are you talking about? I'm not trying to take your position."

"Next time I make a decision, don't go behind my back to get it changed!" The Dean turned, aggressively opened my classroom door, and then slammed it shut.

I stood in the middle of my class, speechless, and realized I went too far.

A day prior, I had another teacher come to me about a problem she was having with a student. The teacher went to the Dean of Students and asked for the student to be placed in In-School Suspension (ISS) for their behavior. Upon the request of the teacher, no consequences were provided by the Dean. The teacher asked if I could ask the Assistant Principal to assign ISS to the student instead. Immediately, I said that I didn't think it was a good idea. With more persuasion and outside of my good judgment, I allowed my ego to get in the way and agreed to speak to the Assistant Principal.

During my off period the next school day, I went to the Dean of Students and shared what occurred in the other teacher's classroom and how the student was acting out. The Dean said they would look into it and I went back to class. After school, I was walking down the main hall and saw the Dean of Students talking with the Assistant Principal in a teacher's classroom. Thinking this was a prime moment to speak to the Assistant Principal, I went into the classroom and brought up the student from the other teacher's classroom.

"Hey, I was wondering if you looked into the student's behavior from our conversation earlier?"

I ran through all the student's transgressions again, hoping for the Assistant Principal to interject.

I turned to the Assistant Principal and asked, "What do you think about the situation?"

The Assistant Principal agreed with my assessment and when I turned back around, I could see that the Dean of Students was upset about the conversation.

The next day the student received consequences and I had the uncomfortable tongue lashing, which I deserved.

Regardless of the outcome, I know I didn't help the situation by getting involved. I stuck my nose where it didn't belong and for that, I got put in my place. I knew I should have allowed those who originally were involved to determine a resolution for the situation. I let my pride and ego get in the way. Instead of letting the Dean of Students work out the situation, I inserted myself to show I could do a better job in the position. With that belief, I circumvented the process to get the outcome I thought was best.

Looking back, I could have positively impacted the situation in other ways. When the teacher came to me with their request, I should have assisted in the area of classroom management, student engagement, or classroom discipline measures. Instead, I focused on an area that was beyond my position. As aspiring leaders, we need to make sure we are assisting for the greater good of everyone involved, not manipulating the system to increase our power. It's easy to try to prove our worth as a leader and lose focus on the task at hand. It's important to be in tune with our intentions so it doesn't distract from the mission or our goals.

Pitfall #2: Picking up the Slack

In addition to being a teacher, I was also a football, basketball, and track coach. There were many days that I was pulled from the classroom or off the field to complete administrative tasks, which, for athletics, left the coaches short-handed. After several years of gaining administrative experience, I could tell that my absence from practice was wearing on them. One morning, I came out to the field during the off-season and asked the Athletic Director (AD) if I could help the administrative team with a project.

Before the AD could respond, one of the other coaches overheard my request and yelled, "Why does it matter? He's never here anyway."

I laughed and turned to see the other coach scowling from across the field. It was obvious he wasn't kidding. I turned back to my AD and he reluctantly said they had it covered.

As I was walking away, my AD said with a smirk, "Hey, you better be an administrator soon."

The next day, my AD asked me to come to the coach's office. I knew exactly why he wanted to talk. I sat down and the coach explained that things needed to change.

"Hey, I understand you have goals and I want you to move up. But, we are all covering for you and picking up your slack. When you leave, it affects us all and this program."

I realized that when I was trying to gain additional administrative experience, it affected everyone else. The other coaches did not sign up for the extra work or get compensated in any way. They covered my absence because they had to, not because they chose to help out. Leaving the classroom or the field to help out the administrators was exhilarating. It was always a new experience that was more exciting than the positions I currently held. However, creating more work for my coworkers was unfair and selfish. I told my AD that moving forward, I would not be absent from my coaching duties to help the administrators. Although I was disappointed in the possibility of missing additional experiences, I knew it was the right decision moving forward.

Pitfall #3: Overconfidence

As I was subbing for the Dean of Students position, my Assistant Principal came to the office to speak about a student's consequences and how the parents needed to be called. My Assistant Principal was holding a small piece of paper out to me with the phone number written on it and said, "I don't know if you want me to call this parent but the father can be...."

Before another word could be spoken, I quickly grabbed the paper and said, "Nope, I got it."

My Assistant Principal smirked and said, "Are you sure because the dad can...."

Again interrupting, I said, "No, I got this."

"Ok, let me know how it goes."

As soon as the Assistant Principal left, I grabbed the phone and began dialing the number. The phone began to ring and I gathered all of the data to share with the father.

Someone picked up the phone and said, "Hello?"

"Hi, my name is Joshua Stamper and I'm the administrative intern."

Before I could say any more, the father said, "An Intern? So you're not a real administrator?"

I quickly tried to explain the position, shared what his child did at school and the consequences assigned.

The father responded, "Yeah, that won't be happening. I don't believe that occurred and there is no way I'm accepting punishment from a pretend administrator. In fact, I think I'll call my lawyer to see if an "intern" can provide any discipline to my child." The phone abruptly went to a dial tone.

I sat there for a moment, trying to determine what had happened and if there was anything I should have said differently. For one thing, I never used the term "administrative intern" after that conversation. I got up from my chair, took a deep breath, and walked to my Assistant Principal's office.

When I arrived, my Assistant Principal looked up and asked, "How did it go?"

I opened my mouth but I really didn't have any words to describe what occurred.

"That good, huh?" My Assistant Principal was smiling ear to ear as he leaned back in his chair.

We both knew that I was cocky and overconfident before the phone conversation.

"Yeah, you may want to call the father back before he calls his lawyer."

My Assistant Principal laughed and said, "I'll give him a call and then we can debrief about your conversation."

The lesson was obvious. Never think that any administrative task is going to be easy, especially a parent phone call about student discipline.

Pitfall #4: Taking it Personal

The last landmine is a difficult one and a lesson I still struggle with sometimes. As a leader, we make a lot of decisions and interact with many people over the course of a day. It's easy to have your feelings hurt or take things personally. One day, I was asked to sub for the Dean of Students, and I had a substitute for my classroom. The substitute teacher's children went to the school, and one of the children used their bike to get to school. The day prior, the student's bike went missing, and the student came to my office to report the missing bike. As I began my investigation, it became obvious that several of my athletes were involved in the missing bike incident. By midday, I had five students involved, no bike, and a lot of lies. I needed a student to start to tell the truth. I called for another athlete that I had a good relationship with to see if I could get him to tell me the truth. As the student was telling me the story, it was obvious he was lying.

"Come on. It's obvious you're lying. What really happened?"

"No, I swear!"

We went back and forth for a few minutes, and finally, I couldn't take the lies anymore. I stood up and yelled, "Are you kidding me?! Why are you lying to me? I already know you're involved. I have five people who told me you were the one who stole the bike! Now, you can tell me the truth to get a lesser consequence, or I can give you additional consequences for lying!"

I could feel my face was bright red from anger. The student began to cry, and he shared that it wasn't him who stole the bike. He was with the students who did. However, the group of students rode the bike back to a friend's house, took the bike apart, and dispersed the bike parts out to each of them. They took the parts and added them to their bikes.

He looked up and said, "I'm sorry I lied, but I didn't steal the bike. I do have some of the parts with me, though."

I couldn't believe what I just heard. All I could say was, "I need you to write this in a statement, and we need to get this bike back in one piece."

After gathering all the students' statements, I called all of the parents, and they were extremely helpful. One parent drove up with the bike and the students gathered all the parts from their bikes that they stole. As a team, they put the bike back together and I was able to return it to the owner that afternoon. I provided consequences to each of the students and they personally apologized to the victim and their parent.

Although I was able to get the bike back together, I was not able to repair the relationship with the student I yelled at. Several weeks later, I overheard the student tell a classmate, "I don't know why Coach Stamper hates me." After class, I told the student that I didn't hate them but I was disappointed by his prior decision.

The student quickly said, "If that is true, then why did you give me the most consequences?"

The more I tried to explain my actions, the more the student didn't believe me. Prior to this incident, we had a solid relationship, but after the negative interaction, it was apparent we were not on good terms. Although the student made a mistake, I took the lies personally instead of looking at them as an independent behavior. In my reflection, I would have communicated differently and provided fewer consequences to the student.

It would be wonderful to say that this was an isolated incident, but I have taken many things personally over the years: anything from negative comments from an upset parent, teacher input about a "worthless" professional development session, or a student telling me that I didn't care about them. The longer I'm in the administrative position, the easier it is to decipher the constructive and valuable feedback provided by those you serve instead of the comments driven by strong emotions. However, there is power in words, and it's hard to not take cutting statements personally.

REFLECTIVE OUTLETS

Over the years, I have realized the importance of reflecting on past decisions and experiences. Although I have made many mistakes as a leader, I have tried many forms of reflection strategies to improve and grow in my craft. As a young leader, I didn't see the value of reflection, but with each school year, I see how important it is to review our past decisions. Here are a few reflective outlets I have used during my time as an administrator.

Building a Community

Having a community of leaders has been the most impactful and beneficial reflection practice that I can suggest. As a campus leader, there are many days you feel alone and unable to share what is occurring on school grounds. On tough days, it's natural to want to share what occurred, reflect on the situation, and gain some immediate feedback. By having an outside group of educational leaders, I can share my struggles and ask questions about solutions. Currently, I am using an application called Voxer to communicate with leaders across the country. Voxer allows you to send an audio or text message to one person or a group of people. It's an extremely powerful and efficient tool for conversations on leadership. If you need a community to reflect with, let me know and I will add you to the "Aspire Leadership Group" on Voxer. The application is free to download on your phone and an accessible way to join a community.

Blogging as a Tool

Hopefully, you gained some value from the stories written in this chapter. The power of written words is important. Blogging is a fantastic way to share past experiences, lessons, or strategies. I remember the first time someone asked me to guest blog on their website. I was scared to death and immediately asked, "Who in the world wants to read what I have to say?" What I realized is many people are interested in the blogs and written assessments of past leadership decisions. It's a learning tool for all involved, both author and reader. Although it may require vulnerability, writing a blog creates a consistent practice to relive past situations, which only helps improve our decision-making in the future.

Drawing Notes

It may be my artistic background, but sometimes I don't have the words to use in my reflection. Drawing pictures is a wonderful outlet to get ideas out and allow you to use your mind differently. Pictures are a powerful tool if used correctly. If you have never tried sketch notes before, it's a way to create notes using drawn pictures with written descriptions to create a page of information. Typically, when I'm drawing a picture, my mind is allowed time to think and construct a complete thought. I can come back to my sketch notes to use them as a launchpad for my reflection, new ideas, and action plan.

Audio Recordings

As I've stated earlier, I don't always enjoy writing down my thoughts. It is much easier to express my ideas verbally than to write them down. Similar to Voxer, you can use your audio recording application on your phone to record your self-reflections. Another audio option is participating in a podcast. I know that creating a podcast may not be for everyone, but there are other options. Have you considered being a guest on a podcast? There are hundreds of educational podcasts in existence and every one of them needs guests. Being interviewed by someone is a profound way to reflect on your previous actions, projects, and experiences. The thought of it is much scarier than the experience. Regardless of your audio preference, going back and listening to a past recording is an effective reflective practice.

———

Making Mistakes as a Leader
By Alicia Ray

Did you know that once you are a leader, you will never make another mistake?

Did you just scratch your head wondering how someone could utter such an absurd statement?

Of course, leaders make mistakes! Daily, if you're lucky; possibly even more so, if you're like me. I have learned (truthfully - am still learning) to be okay with making mistakes because it means that I'm still pushing against the status quo and growing in my profession.

Oftentimes I make the mistake of overextending myself. My fully-flexible Instructional Coach calendar gets filled quickly with co-planning and co-teaching, so I have two calendars that I have always used. One is digital and mobile; the other is physical and located in my office. I'm usually adept at transferring information between calendars and keeping appointments. Sometimes as I'm walking from room to room in the hall, a teacher will ask about availability to brainstorm some new ideas several weeks out, and my digital calendar shows that I'm free, so I will block out time on my digital calendar to co-plan with that teacher. When I get to my office, I transfer that block of time to my physical calendar immediately.

In fact, that very thing happened last semester. Mrs. T wanted me to help brainstorm the transformation of a unit of study on January 21st. A few days later, while standing near my office, Mr. M asked if I could help facilitate a new digital tool in his classroom on January 21st. (I'm sure you see where this is going, right?) I was near the physical calendar, so I just checked there. It still showed that I was free, and so I blocked out time to co-teach with Mr. M. On January 21st, I was in the middle of facilitating a new digital tool in a lesson with Mr. M when I got an email from Mrs. T asking when I would be in her room for our brainstorming session.

Oof! Epic fail! I had completely forgotten to transfer the hallway request to my physical calendar!

Has something like this ever happened to you? What comes next? Immediately following the co-teaching with Mr. M, I gave a face-to-face apology to Mrs. T, fully owning the fact that I had double-booked myself because I neglected to put our planning session on my physical calendar. I assured her that I valued her time and expressed my sincere regret for wasting the time we had set aside to plan. She accepted my apology and we rescheduled our brainstorming session, at which I gave 110% of my focus to our time together. In order to avoid this mistake in the future, I now make it a point to transfer information from one calendar to the other at the end of every single day.

I firmly believe that *good* leaders make mistakes regularly. I believe the leaders that are *worth following* are the ones that own their mistakes - no matter how big or small they may be, apologize as needed, and work with others to move forward, learning from those mistakes. There is so much power in the humility and vulnerability of owning one's mistake. Apologizing acknowledges and validates others' feelings. Creating a plan to prevent the same epic fail from happening again shows perseverance and resilience.

Say, "I messed up; I was wrong," then convey a heartfelt "I'm sorry." Follow up with "How can we move forward and grow from my mistake?" Leaders will make mistakes and fail while fulfilling our roles. It's not the failure that defines the leader, but what the leader chooses to do after the failure that separates the good from the great.

Alicia Ray, Lead Digital Learning and Media Innovation Facilitator, Author, Speaker

———

The Ghost of Blogging Past
By Dr. Sarah Thomas

Short for "weblogging," blogs began to appear in the earlier part of the century. The term was even a contender for the word of the year in 2003 (CNN, 2003). In 2004, CNN also stated,

> So if you haven't already started reading blogs, you should certainly begin doing so....Blogs are a real force; they're not just for geeks anymore.

My own personal foray into blogging began that same year when I started one as an aspiring musical artist. (It is literally a sight for sore eyes, so proceed with caution if you want to check it out: www.sarahjthomas.freeservers.com/Diary.htm.) While largely music-based, it also had random reflections, as well as a bit of my journey to becoming a teacher.

Before blogging, my way to process complex emotions was to write songs. "Good news is that I wrote 2 new songs out of my experiences this week, one of them called Mr. E. and the other one I don't have a title for yet," as I wrote on Monday, May 12, 2004. I maintained this practice a few more years, into my early 30s. However, now, blogging has taken over as my preferred Medium for reflection (pun intended; #spoiler).

Looking back on my first blog, I see glimpses into my past, but also my future (i.e., when I said I wanted to buy stocks...I almost jumped out of my skin seeing that just now, as this is my current obsession). Reflecting and blogging, in some ways, *is a map to show where you are, where you have been, and perhaps where you may go.*

An added benefit is that the public nature of blogging allows others to provide affirmation, pushback, and other perspectives that help us get a clearer picture.

Since this first experiment in 2004, I have shifted focus to more educational topics, with the occasional life experiences thrown in. In the following years, I also learned a bit more about readability and a smidge more about UX (user experience).

First Official Education Blog
I got connected to Twitter in April 2013 and haven't looked back. In September of that year, I decided to begin blogging about education (http://sarahdateechur.blogspot.com). For those who know me well, the tone is a lot more snarky and blunt than my usual demeanor, especially in my first post.

To the naked eye, it may seem as though September's post is displaying signs of overwhelm, although that's not entirely true. This was a coming-of-age post, where I was transitioning into *connected educator* land, and seeking to break ties with Party

Sarah's past. In other words, I was an emerging adult. It was a sort of digital adolescence, fully equipped with rebellion and snark.

A month later, I stepped out of the cocoon after having cut my teeth at my first out-of-area edtech conference, *Edscape*. By now, I was fully immersed in my connections, having met members of my Professional Learning Network (PLN) for the first time. The post was written on October 20, 2013, detailing the experience...now seven years later, I can look back and see some moments that happened that day that ended up having a *Butterfly Effect* type impact on the rest of my career.

One such event was learning about Edcamp NJ the following month. I attended a session by Joe Sanfelipo and Dr. Tony Sinansis, which helped shape my perspective on branding (http://sarahdateechur.blogspot.com/2013/12/branding-da-teechur.html).

Provide Value
When we blog, we are creating content, and therefore contributing to the existing literature and providing value by proxy; however, there is one tip that I try to carry over to most of my posts: leave the reader with some actionable steps. This may seem to conflict with another of my strategies, *write for yourself,* but not if you consider that you might be your reader.

My early blog posts probably didn't get very many reads... I would not be surprised if that number has more than 10xed after the publication of this book. But I read them. I go back sometimes to see how much I have grown, or as a reminder of what to do in similar situations.

The biggest change when I moved to WordPress (https://sarahdateechur.wordpress.com) is that I started doing more posts with takeaways for the reader. These ranged from making walkthrough videos to just blogging about various things I learned through professional development, to studying lessons that life had taught me in the school of hard knocks (LOL luckily, not that hard).

I called this WordPress site home for a long time. There was one year where I even started a Blog360 challenge but only made it to Day 20. This was like a journal, an open study session for the world to participate in.

However, education moves faster than dog years, and soon there was a new platform I wanted to try: Medium. This platform would allow more people to find my blogs, as they are searchable and categorized, as opposed to a standalone platform. So I moved once more.

The Final Frontier
I started using Medium in 2017, importing some of my favorite prior blogs (https://sarahdateechur.medium.com/). I found this space because many of my friends started using it. What I also liked is that there were various series and publications that one could use to divvy out their thoughts. I still have yet to master all the features and functionality. At one point, EduMatch had a Medium account, which may be resurrected one day.

What I like about Medium, again, is that it allows you to categorize blog posts, and sometimes suggests them to readers. You do have the option to monetize, which I do not, but some people make good money from their posts. Personally, I don't see myself as a professional blogger; I'm someone who likes to create something productive out of the mess that is sometimes life. Blogging helps me sort through and make it make sense.

Tips for Blogging

- Write for yourself. The audience will come (maybe).
- Leave the reader with some actionable steps...especially if that reader is you.
- Stay authentic. You are the only person who can tell your story.
- Engage your readers, even if they disagree. This can be a gift, as you might gain more clarity. But don't feed the trolls.
- Use your blogs to time-travel. "Visit" your previous self over previous years and see how far you have come.

As you will note from the timestamps of some entries, throughout the years, I have struggled with getting a full night's sleep. Sometimes the cause was worry, sometimes things that went bump in the night. Sometimes, on a rare occasion, it was the gift of inspiration. At the moment, I didn't always recognize this gift for what it was. However, I started to learn that the best way to flesh out some of my crazier ideas, for better or worse, was to blog about them. I hope that you, too, will use your gift to level up!

Dr. Sarah Thomas, Founder of EduMatch, Author, Podcaster, Regional Technology Coordinator

References
CNN. (2003, December 26). Web site picks year's top word. Retrieved January 01, 2021, from http://www.cnn.com/2003/TECH/internet/12/26/top.word.reut/index.html
CNN. (2004, March 22). The rise of the online citizen. Retrieved January 01, 2021, from https://www.cnn.com/2004/ALLPOLITICS/03/17/polls/

———

CALL TO ACTION:

Regardless of your reflective outlet, it is important to participate in some form of self-assessment. Moving forward to never look back will only allow you to see the possibilities of the future, which will not allow you to grow from the past. For most people, the reflection process is not a natural practice, but it is one of the most important steps in our growth. To be successful, consider the following to enhance the reflection process:

- Schedule time to reflect
- Designate a quiet place
- Construct your thoughts in a journal, blog, sketch note, or audio recording
- Connect with other educators to gain feedback
- Determine what can be improved from the self-assessment

QUESTIONS FOR DISCUSSION

- **Currently, how do you reflect on your leadership practices and experiences?**
- **What outlet are you using to document your past decisions?**
- **What values are important to you to guide you in future decisions?**

Aspire Podcast Resource

Educational Eye Exam
Featuring Alicia Ray

Aspire Podcast Resource

Connecting Educators Globally:
Featuring Dr. Sarah Thomas

6

ASPIRE TO EXECUTE

 "Success doesn't necessarily come from breakthrough innovation but from flawless execution."

— NAVEEN JAIN

READY FOR THE CHALLENGE

After hearing positive feedback from the director during the district principals' meeting, I began to turn my focus on my resume, letter of intent, and interview answers. My last interview experience didn't go well and I was extremely nervous about the process. Thinking about being denied again and having to wait another school year to apply was almost unbearable. I sat down with my principal to discuss how I would answer certain leadership questions in an interview with the district directors. As soon as I started to ask about the interview process, he stopped me. He asked, "When you become a Dean and go to another campus, are you prepared to go to a tougher school?"

At the time, the district stated that a teacher couldn't be promoted to an administrative role on the same campus. And I honestly didn't put much thought into it. My principal, "the strategic leader," explained some of the possible campuses that may have administrative openings in the summer and the areas each campus may need to address. He stated that before I could lead a building, I needed to know who I was and what I stood for. The previous two-and-a-half years, I had a rocky ascension in the building and I knew I had to determine my identity as a leader before I went into an interview and served in another building.

PREPARATION OF DOCUMENTATION

After I created my identity framework and reflected on my leadership accomplishments, I began preparing the documentation needed to apply to become an administrator. I met with my administration team and shared my documentation with them. My principal looked over my resume and immediately identified several formatting items he wanted me to change. His feedback was the following:

Make Your Resume One Page

When my principal was scanning my resume, I had three years of leadership on my campus and in the district. I had begun to accumulate more accomplished tasks, experiences, and programs. As I continued to add items with paragraphs of descriptions to my resume, my resume quickly became a multi-page document. As soon as my principal started flipping through the pages, he looked up and said, "This is way too long. You need to shorten this to one page." He continued to explain that a person needs to be able to scan and catch the highlights of your strengths in a short time. Administrators typically don't have time to sit down and read a four-page resume. The document needs to be concise and to the point, while highlighting your accomplishments.

Easy to Read Format

The other point of improvement provided by my principal was the format didn't allow for the reader to easily access the important experiences and skills quickly. Here are a few resume suggestions provided to me in my meeting with my principal, which are concepts I still share with my campus aspiring leaders:

Don't be afraid of using bullet points

Although it may feel odd, your resume shouldn't be written in paragraph form. You will want to use bullets to allow the reader to gain important information quickly. Bullet points are a great technique to present concise and informative points of interest. Most likely, the person reading the resume will not read every word on the document. It's important to have a format that is easy to navigate so they can find the information they are seeking.

Highlight the most important and relevant accomplishments first

Often, resumes will go in chronological order to the candidate's experience, such as beginning with their college degrees and followed by their positions held. Instead of having your resume as a timeline of experiences, categorize the order by the most important topics. What leadership experiences are most relevant and need to be highlighted? Place those towards the top.

Bold the topics and make sure the format of the document is consistent

To create a professional feel, It's important to have a format that looks clean and consistent. A resume needs to have consistent fonts, sizing, and spacing throughout the document. Bolding the topics assists the reader in finding the important areas and scanning the information quickly.

Once I had the changes to my resume and created a letter of intent, I sent those items to the district office. Within a week, I was asked to interview with the district directors. They stated that since I advanced past the first round the prior year, I did not have to interview with the principal panel again. My only interview would be with the district directors. I knew this was the most important interview of my life and if I messed up again, I wouldn't be provided another opportunity. It was time for me to execute a flawless interview using the leadership experiences, reflective practices, and teachings of my mentors.

SECOND CHANCES ARE INVALUABLE

Once again, I found myself at the district administrative building waiting to go into the conference room for my interview with the district directors. I could feel my stomach turn over as flashes of my first failed interview came rushing over me. As soon as my self-doubt began to intensify, the Director of Secondary Schools came out to greet me. I took a deep breath, stood up, and shared a cheerful greeting. When I entered the conference room, it was set up the same way as my previous interview. The one noticeable difference was the people sitting around the room. As I scanned the room, the directors sitting around the table were different, and they were the exact people I wanted in the interview. This was a good sign. As the interview began, there were three interview techniques that I wanted to implement to help me through the process. I spent a great deal of time reflecting on my interview practices and knew this time I would:

If Offered, Take the Water

This may seem like an odd and simple strategy but I can't tell you how important water was for me in the second interview. My nerves were at an all-time high as I was sitting in the conference room. We all know the importance of water for our health and brain; however, I used the glass of water as a tool to take a moment to breathe and calm my nerves. Whenever I felt anxious, I would pause, take a drink, and then answer the question. Even though I took the occasional moment to take a sip of water, my answers were fluid, clear, and concise.

Give Real Examples

In my first interview, I often gave responses to what I would do as an administrator instead of providing real leadership examples of what I had accomplished on my campus or in the district. I had more examples to use with an additional year of leadership experience, and I was extremely intentional about telling stories of how I positively impacted all stakeholders. Now being on the other side of the table during interviews, I can assure you that everyone at the table wants to know what practical things you have accomplished rather than theory or hypothetical scenarios.

Highlight Yourself

It may be because I'm in education, but I had a difficult time highlighting my accomplishments. During my first interview, I gave a lot of credit to my administrators and peers, even if I was the one who led an initiative. Every time I highlighted any aspect of my leadership, it felt like I was boasting about my accomplishments. It took several meetings with my mentor, as she coached me repeatedly, to help me break through the uncomfortable feeling. In an interview, it's important to speak about your awards, initiatives, and recognitions. Even though it may feel awkward, you need to communicate what you have to offer the school, district, or organization.

As I walked out of the interview, I knew my interview answers had improved dramatically. Due to my prior experience with the district interview process, reflecting on my mistakes, and being coached by my administrative team, I had a good understanding of what was going to be asked and how to structure my answers. When I walked to my car, I was smiling ear to ear. I knew that this positive interview was the last piece of the puzzle to be selected for the administrative pool.

NOT FINISHED YET

A week later, I was called by the central office to inform me that I was selected to be placed in the administrative intern pool, which meant I was eligible to interview at secondary campuses for the Dean of Students position. There were several openings in the district and I knew I had a good chance of being selected for one of the positions. The next day, I received a call from the principal of a middle school in the district. She wanted to know if I was able to come in for an interview after school in the next few days. I was surprised at how fast the process was going, but I was extremely excited about the prospect of advancing to the next level.

When I arrived for the interview at the middle school, it had a very different feel than the district interview. As I walked into the interview in the principal's office, I was shocked to see twelve eager people crammed around the table. It was obvious that this campus was concerned with who was going to be selected for the open administrative position. Many questions were very specific to the position, which was a change from the district questions. I had to quickly change my strategy by answering the questions with more detail on how I was going to address the topics provided. The focus of the questions had to do with student discipline, relationship building, parent conflict, and campus culture. I was thankful I had many leadership experiences on my campus, because I needed every example to help answer their questions. Since I subbed for the Dean of Students often, I had a very good understanding of the responsibilities and processes of the position.

I don't know if it was because I was already in the administrative intern pool, but I was calmer and more collected in the campus interview. When I walked out of the principal's office, I had a great feeling I was going to be offered the position. A few days later, on the last day of school, I received a phone call from the principal offering me the Dean of Students position. I happily accepted and ran down to the front office to tell my administrative team.

After reflecting on the entire process, there are a few important aspects that occurred behind the scenes. Those that were imperative to rise in my leadership journey were:

A Powerful Advocate

After the fact, I found out that there were a lot of conversations that occurred between my principal and the district. If I didn't receive the full support of my principal, I wouldn't have even had a chance to interview for the administrative pool. It's one thing to have an opportunity to get administrative experience on the campus, but you will need a powerful advocate communicating back to the district on your behalf. If your advocate is not your current administrator, make sure you have a leader, who you have worked for, to be your professional reference. It's important to have support from someone in a higher position to increase the chance of having the opportunity to interview.

Networking is Key

If I only remained on my campus to assist in leadership tasks, participate in committees, and experience administrative tasks, I never would have advanced past the teacher leader level. My opportunities changed when I joined district aspiring-leadership events, committees, meetings, and events. It's important to be seen and to build authentic relationships with the leaders who make important decisions. This can be in your district, surrounding districts, or around the country. With the increased role of social media, networking has never been easier. The key is to be genuine, though. If you participate in online or district-based initiatives only to be seen, it will be obvious. Effective networking requires you to put yourself in a place to meet new leaders while working toward the same goals. It is not meant to be purely a self-promotion practice.

Timing is Everything

As I have shared before, when I have my eye on a goal, I want to accomplish it at breakneck speeds. Unfortunately, my timing is not always correct. If I would have been placed in the administrative intern pool one year prior, I would not have gained the opportunities and experiences from my new principal and networked throughout the district. Without the extra year of preparations, I probably would have been less successful in the Dean of Students role, resulting in me staying in that position longer. Although it hurt not being selected to advance and I didn't understand it at the time, it was the best decision for my development. Our self-determined timeline is not always the best for ourselves, the campus, or the district. It's important to seek guidance from multiple sources to identify the correct time to progress in your journey.

Interview the Interviewers

As much as we are interviewing for a position, we need to be interviewing the interviewers. Every job is not the best fit for you. I have been in many interviews where, by the end of the interview, I knew I was not a good fit for the school or district. It is ok to not accept a position if it's not a good fit. There have been several times where I have been brutally honest in my responses because I wanted to push the envelope to see how the interviewees would respond. If they were not going to select me based on who I was and what I believed, I didn't want to be a part of their future. We all need to be in a place where we can grow and be ourselves. At the end of an interview, ask the important questions to get to know the school or district. Make sure it is a place you will be happy to work for a long time.

---

10 Tips for a Successful Interview
By Dr. Jill Siler

I have had interviews that I have absolutely crushed, and others that were so bad that I didn't know whether to laugh or cry. But every time we put ourselves out there, we learn and better prepare ourselves for the next opportunity. Here are my 10 best tips for a successful interview:

My first word to you is to **Celebrate**! The higher your journey takes you, the fewer opportunities there are —so it is increasingly difficult to get that coveted interview. When you have been bestowed an opportunity to interview, take a moment to celebrate!

Hands-down, the most important key to a successful interview is to **Do Your Homework!** One of the main things that will set you apart from others is your knowledge of the organization and the role that you are walking into. Scour their website, analyze the available reports from the state. Look for areas where they are doing AMAZING things and areas where they could grow. Most of all, learn what is important to them!

Dive Deep into your answers. My worst interview was one in which I was asked 21 questions and I finished in about 21 minutes (*not my finest hour*). You don't want to ramble, but you do want to go below the surface on your answers. Our answers need to be about more than the "what" (surface-level information). We need to paint the picture of "how" and "why" we would lead through that situation. The 12 most important inches of leadership are those between your head and your heart.

Along the same lines as going deep, **Lift the Language**. One time I was asked how I evaluate staff. My 60-second answer outlined how we utilized the state evaluation system. Lifting the language is thinking about the core of their question and speaking to that. In a subsequent interview, I shared that while there are frameworks that we use, our job is to help guide people to reflect on where they are and where they want to be and then empower them to get there. And then I spoke very frankly about the very real issue of how to work with people who are struggling. Nothing changed about how I evaluated staff from the 1st interview to the 2nd. I just learned how to talk about it in a way that connected deeply with others.

Tell Your Story. Think about three things that you are proudest of in your current work that you want to share. Then listen for opportunities to speak about that work within the context of one of their questions. You always want to answer questions directly, but there are often ways you can incorporate your proudest work into your answers.

Consider the possibility to **Leave them with Something**. This might be an outline of your core values and include highlights of recent initiatives and how that plays into the strengths and weaknesses of that school organization. It might even be an entry plan for your first 60-90 days on the job. Make sure it, like your resume, is a reflection of the kind of work you will produce on the job.

The interview is not just a one-way look for them to determine whether you are a good fit. It is also a time for you to determine whether they are a good fit for you. It is a time to **Contemplate Marriage**. Don't just focus on getting the job. Focus on having the job. Is this the right position for you; the right organization for you; an opportunity where you will be able to find success; an opportunity where you will be able to fulfill your purpose/your calling; a job where you will be supported and an organization that you fully support?

The interview may officially be over when you walk out of the room, but your work is not done. The **Follow Up** is important! Have "thank you" notes prepared that can be sent immediately and consider a follow-up email as well. Be specific about what you heard that would make you want to work for them and share a sincere word of thanks for the opportunity to be considered. Consider finding someone you know and trust who will allow you to **Do a Dry-Run**. Ask your network for sample interview questions and spend time thinking through your answers reflecting on the tips above. Then find someone who has experience hiring who can lead a practice interview and who will give you explicit feedback.

This goes without saying, but **Be You!** Smile. Let them see your passion. Let them hear your commitment and the purpose from which you do what you do. Let them know that you're not perfect, but that you're reflective, coachable, and take responsibility for when things don't go as you had anticipated. Let them know that you are REAL!

Remember that every interview is an opportunity to learn and grow! Either way, be thankful that you successfully took one more step that will help get you closer to where you ultimately want to go!

Dr. Jill Siler, Superintendent, and Author of *Thrive Through The Five*

———

CALL TO ACTION:

Sending in your documentation and interviewing for a new position is a difficult and time-consuming task. Regardless of how many times you go through the process, it will still be stressful and hard work. Although not all of these strategies may be helpful in your specific situation, the important concept is that you learn from your mistakes, try again, and execute at a higher level. As an administrator, I have witnessed many aspiring leaders fail the principal's exam, not be selected for a position, or have a poor interview, and they walk away from leadership as a whole. We have to understand that we are not meant for every job and we won't be offered every position we apply for. We must continue to improve our practices, network with a larger community, utilize our advocates, and effectively communicate the amazing skills we possess.

QUESTIONS FOR DISCUSSION

- Reflecting on your interview practices, what are some areas that need improvement?
- Who are some important leaders who can advocate for your leadership skills and your advancement?
- How are you networking with educational leaders in your district, surrounding districts, and around the country?

 Aspire Podcast Resource

Overcoming New Challenges:
Featuring Dr. Jill Siler

PART II

CHARACTERISTICS OF LEADERSHIP

Once I transitioned from a teacher to an administrator, I was confronted with a whole new set of challenges. In a very short period of time, I went from an established building leader that knew every aspect of the campus to the "new guy" struggling to grasp the position. Although I won't be sharing an extensive look into each year of my administrative journey, I do want to provide a guide using three important leadership characteristics.

In the second part of *Aspire to Lead*, I want to focus on three characteristics that every educational leader must possess to be successful in their leadership role. Now, by no means are these three qualities the only characteristics a leader should possess. However, I believe that your leadership journey will be fulfilling and long-lasting if you exuberate the characteristics of empathy, passion, and creativity.

———

What Is More Important: Status or Values?
By Jeff Gargas

Your values are a fundamental piece of how you lead. They are the guide by which you measure every decision, every success, and every failure. If you're not clear on what your core values are, that's okay. You do not need to have them figured out right now, today. However, I encourage you to take the time to reflect and deploy critical self-awareness to discover your values.

There are a lot of books, websites, online courses, and podcasts that can help you discover your values. You can find list after list of common values, and these are a great starting point if you're feeling a bit overwhelmed. But to find your true core values, you have to dig deep into your journey so far. What have you done, and why have you done it? Why have you made the decisions you have made to this point? Why did you feel great about one outcome, and devastated by another? What is really driving you? Be honest, critical, and open with yourself. Your values are for you.

But your values are only as good as the action they drive in you. Saying something is important to you is easy. Proving it again and again with the actions you take, takes commitment. If you truly believe in something, you need to commit to it. You need to live by it.

Helping vs Selling
I can smell the wings like they're sitting in front of me. Buffalo Wild Wings' honey BBQ. A heaping basket was full of them. It was 2015, and I was having a mid-afternoon lunch with my friend, Chad Ostrowski.

Chad had reached out to me about creating an ebook to share a new framework he had developed in his classroom. After hearing what The Grid Method had done for him and his students, I convinced him to go into business with me. We wanted to help other teachers impact their students the same way Chad had been able to impact his.

"We're going to give it all away."

"Wait...what? You said we were going to be able to make money with this."

"Yea, we will...someday. Right now, we're going to give it all away for free."

"...ok…"

"I want to make it so that a teacher can come to our site, take the free course, download some resources, read a few blogs, and then be able to effectively implement The Grid Method in his or her classroom, without ever paying us a dime. If we do that correctly for long enough, people will want to pay us, because we'll actually be helping them with this thing you created, not just trying to sell it to them."

Since the very first day of the Teach Better Team, one of our core values has been to help people, not sell them. Now, this is not an uncommon value for a business to have. In fact, you'll likely find something similar in a lot of marketing plans across a wide variety of industries. The difference that I've found is in the execution of that value.

You see, the "help vs sell" mentality is nothing new. It has been the cornerstone of strong content marketing plans for years. However, even though many companies claim it to be a core value of theirs, they struggle with actually following through with it. What I've found, and what we believe at Teach Better, is that this concept, this value, cannot be something that is a marketing strategy for us (even though it is a great marketing strategy). It needs to be more. It needs to go from "a strategy we use" to "how we do things."

We don't just claim to want to help teachers, or to put people above profit; we live it.

Think through your values. Are they important enough for you to put all of your faith in their guidance of future decisions? Do they truly drive you? Are they more important than a paycheck, a title, or a status?

If you've struggled with decisions, or worried about what path you should take, turn to your values. Execute those values; not for the potential monetary gain or career capital, but the mission. For your mission, your purpose.

Find those values. Let them guide you.

Jeff Gargas, COO/ Co-Founder of Teach Better, Co-Author of *Teach Better* and Co-Host of *Teach Better Talk Podcast*

Aspire Podcast Resource

Teach Better to Lead Better:
Featuring Jeff Gargas

7

EMPATHY AS A LEADER

 *"**Empathy** is being concerned about the human being, not just their output."*

— SIMON SINEK

WELCOME TO A NEW CAMPUS

*W*hen I was hired as the Dean of Students, I thought I had it all figured out. I had a ton of experience in the position at my last campus and served in the role many times as a substitute. In my mind, this was going to be an easy and smooth transition.

At the beginning of the school year, one of my first tasks was to present to my new staff on the discipline policies and procedures. When I began to go through my slideshow of the student handbook and discipline plan, I could feel the staff had many questions from the material I was presenting. Once I was done, I asked if anyone had questions. As soon as I said that, most of the room's hands shot up. One after one, the teachers asked:

- "If a student misbehaves and is disruptive, can I send them to your office?"
- "What are you going to do if a student skips my class?"
- "If a student gets into a fight, what will be their punishment? Will they come back to my class?"
- "So if a kid is absent a bunch, are you going to take them to court?"

The questions kept coming and it was obvious there was a concern with student behavior on the campus and whether I was able to do the job. I assured them that I would take care of everything and provided examples of discipline I dealt with at my last campus. I desperately wanted the staff to believe in my skills. By the end of the presentation, I had the teachers clapping and they were coming up afterward telling me how relieved they were to have me on campus. I thought everyone's response was odd, but I didn't know why.

DIFFERENT SCHOOL WITH DIFFERENT NEEDS

It didn't take long to understand the concern of the staff. On the first day of school, I was conducting lunch duty and I looked over to see a student stand up and punch another student in the face. At my previous campus, we rarely had student fights, so I was shocked at what I saw. I rushed over to stop the conflict and asked the student to come back to my office.

When I walked with the student back to my office, I asked, "Why did you punch that student?"

The student, still very upset, said, "He touched my pizza."

After discussing what occurred in the lunchroom and a little about the student's background, it was evident that food was a large trigger for the student. He came from a household where he didn't know if he was going to have a meal and the food he received at school was often the only food he ate. Someone taking his food wasn't a sign of comedy; it was a threat to survival. On day one of the new school year, it was evident that the students and the community had very different needs than my last school.

As the school year continued, the student infractions increased. Each day, I had a line of students out of my office door and I was constantly assigning students with in-school or out-of-school suspensions. I was called often to a classroom to escalate an interaction between a teacher and the student. Many students were sent out of class for "disrespect" or "disruption to the learning environment." The referrals piled up and I was completely overwhelmed. It didn't matter how many times I suspended a student, their behaviors did not improve. Throughout the school year, students were being sent to the alternative school, arrested, or expelled for their actions. It was the most stressful year in my educational career and I wanted to walk away from education. I felt like a complete failure. Something needed to change, but I didn't know where to begin.

FOSTER CARE TRAINING

Around that time, my wife and I became foster parents. We had two biological children and felt we had the capacity to provide a safe and loving home to children in foster care while their parents worked towards reunification. To become foster parents and ongoing, to maintain our license, we were required to attend a large amount of training.

At the end of that school year, we had our annual mandatory foster care training. I wasn't very excited to attend because, often, the courses had the same information, activities, and instructor. The trainer went through their usual information and, to my surprise, changed up the routine. They stated that we were going to learn about trauma-informed practices utilizing a program that was constructed at Texas Christian University (TCU). The trainer put in the DVD and right away, I knew this was going to be impactful information.

As I was listening to the TCU speakers share about the effects of trauma and using behavior management techniques, I kept thinking about the behaviors I was seeing on my new campus. With each student infraction, I kept sending them away and assuming that the punishment was going to magically fix the behavior. Instead, it created contempt and unresolved problems. During the entire course, I kept wondering, "How can I address the student's behavior in the classroom while keeping the relationships intact?" I knew there was a better way than what I was experiencing.

As teachers, we are trained in nonverbal communication, which helps us determine if students are engaged in the lesson, confused by the material taught, or lacking the full depth of understanding. We use these skills to modify teaching strategies, assessments, and curriculum every day. What would happen if we applied the same skills to our assessment of and responses towards negative behavior as we do to learning? Oftentimes, after a student misbehaves, the student is removed from the learning environment. Similar to a "time-out," the student is placed in a new environment and disconnected from the class. Most times, someone other than the teacher speaks to the student about their negative behavior and provides a consequence. When the student is allowed to return to the learning environment, the relationship with the teacher and other students is fractured and unrestored due to the removal process.

As I witnessed this cycle in my school, I realized we needed to add some additional tools to our toolbox. During the school year, I assembled an amazing group of teachers to create the "Relationship Action Team" (The RATs). We didn't know much about the topics of trauma-informed or restorative practices, but we were willing to learn, build, and implement a new system of strategies. As a group, we had to determine what our goal was for student behavior and how we were going to create safe, healthy, and authentic interactions with our students. If a student doesn't believe you care about them, then the response to redirection or correction will become defensive. To begin the process, we needed to adjust how we conducted our classroom practices and how we interacted with students. When a student wasn't conducting themselves appropriately or displayed anger, teachers began using a form of a "time-in" and de-escalate strategies. Once the student was calm and ready to engage, teachers provided opportunities for students to conduct "redos." Oftentimes, it became a teaching moment to model and share the appropriate actions and communication. The student was provided with another opportunity to try again and stay in the learning environment.

In addition, we decided to implement social-emotional practices in the classroom to establish healthy student relationships, provide opportunities for safe communication, and teach appropriate student behavior. To assist in this goal, the Relationship Action Team learned about a proactive and reactive system called Restorative Practices. The philosophy and core belief of restorative practices is to build healthy relationships while restoring the harm caused by the student's decisions and actions. By creating healthy relationships and positive interactions, we were able to reduce harmful behavior by providing clear expectations, modeling appropriate communication, and creating safe environments. If students were in conflict, restorative practices provided a system to repair harm, restore relationships, resolve conflict, and establish responsibility and ownership. The four practices learned and implemented were relationship circles, restorative circles, relationship agreements, and reflection activities.

Relationship Circles

As a proactive measure, in the classroom, teachers utilize "relationship circles" to allow every student an opportunity to share in a safe space. To construct a relationship circle, each student positions themselves in a circle, the teacher is the moderator, and the only person who is allowed to speak is the person holding the "talking object," which usually is a classroom item. With the structure of one person talking and everyone else listening, this allows the students to feel a sense of empowerment, inclusiveness, and belonging within a controlled setting. The questions vary but usually, the questions are geared toward allowing the students to share about non-threatening or non-emotional subjects. For instance, "What is your favorite soda?" or "What sport do you enjoy playing?" This process allows the students to share about themselves, creating connections with other classmates and a stronger bond as a group.

Restorative Circles

By using the relationship circles, the students are taught the basic structure of the "circle." In a restorative circle, the function and structure are the same as the relationship circle. The teacher is the facilitator, and the one holding the "talking object" is the person who is allowed to speak. The difference is the restorative circle is in response to a fractured relationship. It's intended to resolve the conflict and restore the relationship. In the restorative circle, it is important to establish three rules:

1. Only speak if you have the "talking object" to establish safety.
2. Be honest and stick to the facts.
3. Speak without using attacking language towards the other people involved in the circle.

As a facilitator, it is important to remind the students of these rules as it is extremely natural for students to speak about the actions of others before looking at their own actions. This structured process provides students with a healthy model for reflection, problem-solving, and conflict resolution.

Collective Agreements

The collective agreements are a collaborative activity with the class or select group of students to create shared expectations among all parties (student-to-student, teacher-to-student, and/or student-to-teacher). The agreement is created to provide the students with an opportunity to have input and ownership in the expectations. The agreement is a working document, which can be changed and modified throughout the year. The teachers have posters on the wall or laminated agreement sheets posted on the student desks as daily reminders for the students and the teacher. Many days, the students respectfully police themselves by pointing out that another student's behavior or interaction isn't meeting the collective agreement.

. . .

Reflection Activities

The reflection activity is a series of questions for the student to answer verbally or in writing after a student participates in unhealthy behaviors. The activity is meant to allow the student to see the effects of their choices, how their actions impacted others, and how the other parties involved felt after the interaction. Often, when a student acts inappropriately, we ask, "What were you thinking?" or "Why would you do that?" Instead, we need to be intentional about asking reflective questions to allow students an opportunity to take ownership of their actions, see the effects of the behavior, and develop a plan to rectify the damaged relationships.

Educators have to consider a student's problematic behavior by looking at the symptoms. Negative behavior is a symptom of a larger problem, which is deeply rooted in a student's social and emotional health. When students have escalating emotions, which result in negative behaviors, we must model composure, not mirror chaos. Each student is different and has very different experiences in life. We can not assume that each child understands or knows how to interact appropriately with adults or authority. Our tactics with student behavior must be differentiated, the same as we do with academics. If we view behavior as a form of communication instead of a personal quality, the misbehavior has a purposeful function related to an unmet need. Behavior is a form of communication, and we cannot enhance learning without improving the emotional wellbeing of the heart.

STRATEGIES OF COMMUNICATION

It's easy to assume that each child comes from a stable situation at home, but unfortunately, many children have been exposed to or are living through horrific situations. When interacting with students you don't know or have an established relationship with, use the following techniques to assist in student management to develop trust and a positive relationship.

Low Tone and Volume of Voice

The tone and volume of your voice can drastically change the dynamics of a conversation or interaction. In a typically developed brain, raising your voice may get the attention of a child, but in a trauma-developed brain, raising your voice is a sign of danger. If I raise my voice to a student with whom I don't have a relationship, most times, the student will begin to use their fight, flight, or freeze survival strategies. In all interactions, utilize a low and controlled tone of voice to provide a calm response to student behavior. The goal should always be to de-escalate the situation instead of releasing our own emotions, which may include anger and frustration.

Proximity to the Student

It is quite natural to correct students' behavior by using close proximity. However, when communicating with a student who has experienced trauma, it is important to make sure you don't get too close or move too quickly toward the child. We need to be mindful of our non-verbals and our spatial awareness to disarm fear. Getting too close to a student in a fight or flight situation will only increase the survival response. In addition to the proximity of space, we need to be mindful of the proximity of height. Instead of standing over a student during an interaction, which may scare or intimidate the child, try to get down to the same level as the student. Bending down, taking a seat, or kneeling allows a child to feel safe and empowered in the situation.

Avoid Power Struggles

Students who have experienced trauma have a redefined perception of safety, danger cues, and trust, which will lead to seeking control of other situations. It is important to understand that the child is trying to protect themselves, and their behavior is a direct reflection of this fear. Many times, as I am in a hurry or being pulled in many directions, I fall into the trap of thinking "I am the adult" or "they just need to do what I tell them," but it's very important to take the time to meet the student at their own needs. Avoid disempowering the student through clear expectations, respectful communication, and consistent actions.

Give Options

Throughout a school day, a student is told to do something hundreds of times. For students who live in a traumatic environment, they feel like they don't have control of their life and the events that occur. By providing options in the classroom and during conversations, we are allowing the student an opportunity to have a small piece of control over the situation. As the adult, you are not giving up control of the situation, since you are the one providing the options for the students, but you are allowing the student the chance to experience a small amount of control in the situation. This strategy builds trust and allows the student a chance to have the autonomy to decide what is best for them at the moment.

Be a Window, Not a Mirror

After going through multiple training sessions to learn about trauma-informed strategies, it became obvious that many of the staff members on my campus were constantly reacting to behavior instead of de-escalating, repairing, and teaching the correct behavior. This was evident when I was called to a classroom to gather a student. As I opened the classroom door, the teacher was behind their desk, yelling across the room at the student. The volume and tone of the teacher's voice were so jarring that I missed what the teacher said. I quickly scanned the room to see it was empty except for the teacher and a student.

I looked at the student and asked, "Are you ok?"

The student looked extremely angry but stated, "Yes, sir."

As soon as the teacher saw me, they began to yell at me about how they felt threatened by the student. I looked at the student and looked back at the teacher. I was extremely confused by this comment. The student was a good 15 feet away from the teacher and there was a class set of desks between them. Although I could tell that the student was upset, there was no evidence that the student was a threat to anyone.

I replied, "This student?" and pointed to the student near me.

"Yes and I'm about to call the cops to report them," the teacher yelled.

Surprised by her statement, I said, "I'll take them and we will figure this whole thing out."

The teacher looked annoyed with my response. "I'm not kidding! I'll call the cops!"

"Ok, go ahead. It's within your right to call the cops. I'm going to take the student to my office and you can tell the police they can find us there." I turned and asked the student to come with me. The student complied and we went to my office.

I was so frustrated and disappointed with the whole encounter. I knew the teacher and student had a good working relationship in the past and this event broke that bond forever. The student had experienced trauma in their past and it was evident that the student was about to have a fight, flight, or freeze response based on the negative interaction. As adults, we have to model the correct way to communicate, especially when we are angry.

EMPATHY IS NOT A WEAKNESS

Historically, schools have focused on the punishment of student behavior, which ignores finding solutions for students' mental health and often causes further trauma. Thankfully, many schools are now finding ways to incorporate restorative practices and social/emotional learning in the classrooms. We must continue to focus on connecting and empowering our students by modeling, facilitating, and developing positive relationships. As educational leaders, it is our responsibility to explore alternative strategies to break the cycle of trauma instead of relying on traditional approaches.

Empathy allows us to look beyond the behavior to determine the true problem. Students won't be able to grow academically or see their full potential until they consistently feel safe, respected, and loved. Empathy is not a weakness but a strength to view and understand the depth of the other person's feelings. As leaders, we have to constantly work on building relationships, modeling healthy communication, and teaching the correct behavior.

————

Two Choices of Empathy
By Nathan Maynard

There are always two choices. We can seek empathy or we create assumptions for context. This is out of our necessity to respond to the context, especially in a leadership role with the students and staff we serve.

I have used restorative practices to help me develop empathy throughout my professional career and personal life. I've also utilized restorative practices with student and staff support through both the proactive and reactive approaches as a building leader. I'm going to dive into one of the strongest components of restorative practices—developing empathy. We have to remember that seeking out empathy is a process that we must be cautious with. Think about a time where you opened up to someone, really felt vulnerable, and how you felt during that. It's scary and takes so much trust to open up to someone. We have to understand that when someone opens up, we are then tasked with two steps— responsibility now that this person trusts us and using grace to teach. When we have empathy, we can creatively problem-solve together and truly meet needs. Punitive reactions and assumptions to context do not give us these opportunities.

As a leader in a school building, we are tasked with maintaining physical and emotional safety for staff and students. We've likely come in contact with a situation where harm was caused to a rela- tionship. These situations give us amazing opportunities to utilize the power of empathy for learning. I'm going to share a situation where I had a staff member cause emotional harm to a student. It was a learning opportunity on both sides and, as a team, we were able to utilize restorative practices to help repair and establish a strong relationship after. I have changed their names for anonymity purposes.

Tay came into my office yelling, "Suspend me! I don't care." Right behind her came Mrs. Lange, clearly frustrated. I asked them to both have a seat, we all did a couple of deep breaths, and then I asked, "Who wants to start—what happened?" Mrs. Lange started and explained that she thought Tay was the one that threw food in the cafeteria and asked her to leave. As Mrs. Lange was explaining, Tay's leg was shaking and she kept shaking her head 'no' and sighing heavily. Tay then said, "Okay, can I tell you what REALLY happened?" Mrs. Lange snickered slightly and shook her head 'no.' Tay then explained that someone threw food, and Mrs. Lange accused her by yelling loudly at her in the cafeteria. Tay said, "You don't remember YELLING. 'Get out of here now, Tay, and go see Mr. Maynard!' Do you?!" Mrs. Lange said, "I did not yell that." Tay then snickered and shook her head, and Mrs. Lange responded to me, "See, this is the attitude that I am honestly getting sick of." Tay stood up and walked out of my office, slamming the door, and walked to the front office to sit by the receptionist. I told Mrs. Lange that I would follow up in a bit, and I went to check on Tay.

I was able to have Tay come back to my office to discuss the situation, just the two of us. Tay began to cry and went into several additional situations where she felt targeted by Mrs. Lange. She said, "I'm just tired of her yelling at me!" I knew that it is inappropriate for any staff member to ever raise their voice at a student, but I did not go into that yet in the conversation. I continued to get context from the situations and took notes. I then asked questions to seek to understand how Tay feels when these situations happen, driving empathy understanding that will be utilized later. I let Tay know how I appreciate her being so open with me, and I let her know that I would like some time to look into the situation in the cafeteria and other ones mentioned. I told Tay I would follow up with her later that day, and I asked her if she would be comfortable with another meeting with Mrs. Lange later. It took some persuading of the benefits and clarifying expectations, for both of them, for the next meeting. Tay agreed. Next, I looked into the situation by watching the video cameras in the cafeteria and found that Tay was not the food-throwing culprit. I also was able to see and hear Mrs. Lange's approach, which was not appropriate to the culture of our building or the way we respect our students' dignity. I found a time when Mrs. Lange was available. She had some silent reading in her class and had another administrator watch her class, so we could speak about the situation. I started off and let her watch the video, where she quickly said, "It was a mistake, but I couldn't see all the other students in the back." We continued to speak, and I let Mrs. Lange know what concerned me more was the approach than even the wrongly assuming. I let her watch a second time, paying attention to her response to Tay. I let Mrs. Lange know that the way she responded made me feel uncomfortable and disappointed, and Tay was harmed by this. Mrs. Lange admitted that she was in the wrong with that approach and asked for coaching. We went through some coaching on this situation, and I also asked Mrs. Lange how she believes Tay must have felt in that situation. She gave some ideas of how Tay must be feeling, which was pretty accurate from my conversation with Tay. I then asked Mrs. Lange what she felt could help repair the harm that she caused, and she suggested that she speak to Tay (which was always my intention, but this is a 'with' process). I also told Mrs. Lange that Tay has reported some other situations that she felt didn't go the best with their relationship together, without going into the details. I let Mrs. Lange know that Tay feels hurt, and we want Tay to feel like she belongs in our school—Mrs. Lange agreed.

Mrs. Lange, Tay, and I had an impactful circle to address the situation in the cafeteria and other situations in their relationships. Mrs. Lange started with an apology to Tay and how she believes Tay must feel. Tay then spoke and accepted her apology with tears in her eyes, saying, "But it's embarrassing." Mrs. Lange explained how that was never her intention, and she will definitely not yell or speak loudly like that to Tay again or other students. They continued to take turns talking about the situation and driving empathy for one another. Tay understood how Mrs. Lange might have felt with some of the past interactions that the two have had. After the conversation naturally felt over, about 10 minutes later, I asked Tay, "What do you need from Mrs. Lange for this situation to be over?" Tay said, "Just to keep her word." Mrs. Lange said, "Of course, Tay. I am sorry."

Tay graduated two years later. Each student put one staff member that helped them the most in their high school journey in the yearbook under their quote—Tay put Mrs. Lange. By utilizing empathy instead of punishment—we were able to not just repair the situation but create a lasting impactful relationship.

Nathan Maynard, co-author of *Hacking School Discipline* and co-founder of BehaviorFlip

———

CALL TO ACTION:

Regardless of your educational title, it's important to review your discipline policy and practices to determine how they are creating an environment of empathy, compassion, and accountability. In my experience, campuses typically continue their discipline procedures from year to year without review, reflection, or change. We cannot be stagnant or rely on traditional practices when it comes to the emotional and behavioral needs of our students. If we view behavior as a form of communication, our students are telling us a great deal. The students who are misbehaving are hurt, broken, and in need of love, safety, and attention. Find ways to restore relationships, teach the correct behavior, and model healthy communication.

QUESTIONS FOR DISCUSSION USING THE ASPIRE MODEL

- *Activate:* How can you show empathy to your students each day?
- *Support:* Which trauma-informed communication strategies can your campus or district utilize to make sure all stakeholders feel safe in the organization?
- *Persevere:* When restorative practices take time and require your emotional capacity, how are you going to persist in the process?
- *Identify:* What procedures, strategies, or resources do you possess that may be able to identify student trauma?
- *Reflect:* What are some unique discipline practices you have implemented to teach student behavior rather than punish them?
- *Execute:* How may you show empathy in your leadership practices to create impactful relationships?

Aspire Podcast Resource

Hacking School Discipline:
Featuring Nathan Maynard

8

EXPANDING YOUR PASSION

"Passion makes us stronger than we are. Love makes us better than we are. Be passionate about the things you love."

— **GALEN WATSON**

EXPERIENCING BURNOUT

For those who experienced a form of professional fatigue or burnout, you know how difficult it is to be motivated to continue in your current role. As an assistant principal, I had many tasks delegated to me, frequently in difficult areas. Student discipline was my duty, and I wanted to break out and learn more in other areas of the position. I felt like I had a good grasp on my assigned tasks and I wanted to be challenged in other ways. In addition to the repetitive nature of the job, I was attempting to advance to the next level in my career. In the prior summer, I had two interviews for a principal job and the interview process did not go well. Without advancement to the next level, I felt discouraged, stagnant, and trapped. It was at this time that I began to search for inspiration.

INSPIRATION THROUGH SOCIAL MEDIA

One morning as I was walking through the hall during the passing period, I was stopped by a teacher. During our conversation, the teacher asked if I ever joined Twitter chats. I told her that I had joined one or two before but I mostly just lurked around Twitter. At this time in my career, I was not very active on social media. The teacher continued to ask me if I followed a list of educators. Her list was endless. Names were flying out of her mouth and many of the educators she listed were authors, such as Dave Burgess, Trevor MacKenzie, and Todd Whitaker. I told her that I would check them out later, but internally, I was thinking I really didn't have time to be on social media. Days later, the same teacher stopped me in the hall and asked again if I joined any Twitter chats. The teacher told me that she was on #LeadUpChat and she learned so much from the educators who were participating. Based on the passion in her voice and her relentless pursuit to get me connected online, I decided I would check it out.

The next week, I went from a Twitter "bystander " to a full-on "participant." What I discovered was a structured thirty- to sixty-minute timeframe to reflect on my own practices, which was exactly what I needed. Similar to what I shared in the *Aspire to Reflect* chapter, I was searching to find an opportunity to designate time for the reflective practice, and Twitter chats provided that opportunity. In addition, I found a really supportive and knowledgeable community of educators. The teachers, counselors, and administrators who were participating in these chats stretched my beliefs, provided unique solutions, and offered new resources to explore. My network began to expand and I learned about blogs, articles, podcasts, and books I never knew existed. I never thought Twitter would be considered an educational resource, let alone an inspiration. It was exactly what I needed to motivate me to be a better leader.

PROFESSIONAL LEARNING NETWORK

As I was posting more on Twitter, I was connecting with more educators around the world and discovering many were speaking at conferences in my area. During that same year, my district invited several administrators, including myself, to attend the state technology conference, and I couldn't wait to go.

Before I left for the conference, the teacher who was so adamant about me participating in Twitter chats said, "You are going to the state conference? You have to go to Todd Nesloney's session. He's the co-author of *Kids Deserve It* and Todd is amazing!" I laughed and told her that I would try and go to his session.

Once I was at the conference, I was blown away by the educators I saw. Eric Sheninger, Alice Keeler, Todd Nesloney, Matt Miller, Amber Teamann, and Aaron Hogan each had amazing sessions, and I was able to connect with most of them at the conference. It's one thing to learn from someone on Twitter, but it's another to be with the person to have a direct conversation about technology tricks, student engagement strategies, blogging, or creating creative learning environments for students. Most of the connections I made at that conference years ago, both presenters and attendees, continue today, and are some of my strongest relationships I have created in my professional learning network.

When I started participating on Twitter, I had no idea what I was building. Now, my online professional learning network is one of the most powerful and influential educational resources I possess. In addition to learning, the support and encouragement I receive from other educators in trials or celebrations are invaluable. The relationships I have created enhance my skills as a leader each day.

DISCOVERING YOUR PASSION

In my second year as an Assistant Principal, I was called into my principal's office to discuss a new opportunity. As I sat down, my principal stated that I was going to be assisting in the creation of an aspiring leadership program for the west side of the district. My first response was,

"Really? Do I need to be a part of another committee?" After hearing more about the new pilot program, I realized that it may be a good experience to build an aspiring leadership cadre.

At the first planning meeting for the cadre, five secondary assistant principals and myself were provided with the vision of the program, which was to provide new experiences and information to potential future leaders. Each participant of the cadre was selected by their building principal and there weren't any qualifications needed to be a member of the program. The idea was to search for individuals with an expressed interest in leadership and provide them with learning or growth opportunities. As a district, there wasn't a leadership development program in place and we were losing quality leadership candidates to neighboring school districts. The aspiring leadership cadre was constructed to build up the talent from within and prepare the participants of the program for greater opportunities on their campus or within the district.

We wanted to build an experience that was unique, challenging, and informative. The cadre provided simulations of leadership experiences, panel discussions with current district leaders, book studies, practicing leadership tasks, and campus visits. After two years of the program's existence, the district informed us that they had created a formal, district-wide leadership development program, and the cadre was no longer needed. Although we were disappointed our services were not needed, we were proud of the work we did in those two years.

Following the ending of the cadre project, I felt like I was missing something. I couldn't put my finger on it, but I knew I wasn't as joyful as I had been in years past. After speaking with my principal about it, I came to the conclusion that I missed helping aspiring leaders. During the same year, I joined our district's Principal Association and I asked if I could create a one-night event for aspiring leaders. They agreed and I started working on the plans. The event was one night with similar concepts to our Aspiring Leadership Cadre. With little advertising, there were 150 attendees from the district. The event went very well as the participants were able to ask questions to a panel of principals, participate in a leadership simulation, and collaborate with their peers in a mock interview. After the event, I had many people ask for more sessions, and it was extremely apparent that a lot of people were seeking more information about leadership. If my district had this many people come to one event with minimal advertising, then how many people were seeking leadership information in surrounding districts, the state, or the country? I knew there were aspiring leaders seeking help with little to no guidance on their campus. If you don't have a mentor, where do you go to gain knowledge, wisdom, or experience? I couldn't stop helping young leaders because the cadre was dissolved or the event had ended. The question became, *how can I help more aspiring leaders?*

FINDING YOUR OUTLET

Later in the year, I had the opportunity to visit Todd Nesloney at his elementary school. As I arrived in the afternoon, Todd was conducting a podcast interview in his office. I sat down to watch and my fascination grew. As soon as he was done with the interview, I launched question after question at him about the process. How do you record the show? Where do you post the audio? How do you get a guest to agree to be on the show? Todd answered all of my questions and explained every aspect of their podcast. I hadn't really listened to many podcasts, outside of the occasional sports show.

Finally, I asked, "I wonder if I could do a podcast for aspiring leaders?" I continued to share how I really missed the program I'd helped create and assisting educators grow in their leadership experience.

Todd grinned and said, "You totally should do it."

The excitement from our conversation expanded as I thought of the impact I may have on other educators seeking information. As soon as I got home, I began to research how to record on YouTube, microphones to purchase, podcast hosting sites, and free audio editors.

Although I was excited about the new project, I was really nervous about the process and sharing my voice with other people. I turned to my friend, Jeff Veal, to ask for his advice. We got together for a Saturday morning breakfast and discussed the potential of the podcast. Jeff was an amazing sounding board and provided so much direction to my original vision. The confidence Jeff provided through our conversation was the tipping point of contemplating the project to creating the podcast.

PASSION PROJECTS

As I shared, prior to my passion project, I was feeling run down and unexcited about my job. I was in my fourth year as an administrator and I wasn't feeling excited to go to work. Something needed to change so I could regain my motivation and feel inspired once again. As I reflected on my role as a leader, it was apparent that my current actions revolved around daily duties and busy work instead of the things I value the most. Through the everyday routines, a question arose:

Has my energy and time been spent improving initiatives that I believe in and am passionate about?

In review, it was apparent that my habits were constructed on managing and responding to inconsequential demands. The focus was on the immediate tasks and the operational functions of the campus instead of participating in activities of conviction and devotion. We all have responsibilities and requirements; however, our lives desire a sense of purpose, which positively impacts the environment around us.

As an educator, we get pulled in a million different directions. Each day, it is far too easy to be sidetracked, interrupted, and derailed from our intended actions and planned events.

How do we combat the busyness of everyday life to work on the things we value the most?

In the discovery and maturation of our "Passion Projects," valuable time and energy are required to develop and contribute to our core beliefs. Establishing healthy habits are crucial in constructing a system to provide the needed attention to grow our ambitions. As I have built my project, there have been three essential aspects, which create a circular process, to cultivate our passions.

1. Rediscover Our Why

With the daily routines, I lost my focus on why I was in education.

Through personal self-review, we are able to assess our past experiences to determine the strengths and weaknesses of the motives of our actions. During this stage, we're able to identify the areas of change, set a direction, and recommit to our values. To discover our "why," we must continuously review, analyze, and examine our beliefs and passions. It was obvious I had lost my passion and I needed to find a way to rekindle the fire burning inside me.

2. **Create**

When we are passionate about an idea, there is a strong desire to plan, design, and create. As we focus on what we find important, producing things we love is not viewed as work. Instead, our desire is to solve problems, construct innovative concepts, and improve prior projects. During the creative stage, the largest obstacle is our focus and discipline of our time. Too often, I have found my attention and time drawn away by unimportant distractions. To establish consistency, it is imperative to develop a habit to guard your schedule and designate a certain amount of time each day to create.

3. **Share**

After we create, it is important to share our work and ideas with others. Through the sharing process, we are able to gain feedback, connect with our community, and inspire others to improve on their practices. As we share, we place ourselves in a state of vulnerability with the chance of criticism. Although criticism is difficult to hear, it allows us to be challenged and pushed to grow further through reflection.

As we experience the cycle of passion, our purpose and inspiration will flourish in our habits and production. I encourage each of us to find our "Passion Project" each day.

———

Expanding Your Passion Beyond Your Job
By Jeff Veal

I am always impressed by our profession of educators who demonstrate a high commitment to ensure that others receive what they need, whether it be creating "aha moments" or filling another person's emotional tank. By nature, as educators, we often are found making personal sacrifices for the betterment of others, going above and beyond; this is what makes this calling so special. As educators, we connect at an intense level with providing for others; this is part of our hard-wiring!

However, if we are not careful, the very things that bring so much joy can slowly become all-consuming, a 24/7 preoccupation with being "in the work." At first, we tell ourselves we can maintain that momentum; it may feel rewarding because you see the quick results. No one intentionally plans to arrive at a place of burnout, but research has shown us that many of our fellow educators leave after just 5 years of being in the profession. Of course, many factors contribute to this unfortunate reality, but one significant factor is losing one's sense of self for the cause. If we want to avoid ending up with a myopic focus on our profession, we have to expand our passion beyond the schoolhouse, starting with these four imperatives.

Commit to Redeem the Time
Yes, taking personal time might seem counterintuitive since educators are wired to give of themselves. As an educational leader, I believe strongly in this truism, "you can not take others where you have not first been." We have all told others to take care of themselves while neglecting our own mental or physical care. If you want to lead others, it begins by ensuring your tank is full. Consider what is a passion, a hobby, that is life-giving that you have since long neglected...life doesn't happen by looking in the rearview mirror. You have to make a decision to reclaim time;

there is no such thing as finding extra time —you have to redeem it.

Likewise, be known as a gracious permission giver of others; create conditions that create margin for yourself and others. If you are a building leader, it could begin by canceling a school faculty meeting, encouraging personalized learning opportunities that are interest-driven, and giving time back into the hands of our staff. When students and teachers are given "space" or time, they are free to engage, explore, and experiment in what gives life outside of our profession.

Communicate Your Boundaries

In the process of giving your all to students or your staff, don't give it all away, or you will have nothing left. Setting margins, those moments to recharge, and reflect are crucial for you—plus your family and friends need you too! Practically, set boundaries on your professional email, calls, and texting by taking care of those before leaving for the day and then communicate that expectation to others—this includes shutting it off on weekends! Learn to say no with your boundaries; it may be the most important two-letter word you start to exercise.

Connection Over Comfort

As an edleader for a campus or teacher leader, model the way by seeking out your adventure and discover personal new opportunities that create pathways of learning, curiosity, and creativity. As you learn, bring those opportunities back to your people that will elevate the journey for your team. Be curious about your people. Our people need to see us as the most curious learner in the building. Get out of your "edbubble"— go and learn! How? Leveraging technology tools through edchats found on Twitter or webinars is an easy way to expand your learning and create meaningful connections in the process. Being a connected learner and leader can be transformational for fueling your passions.

Celebrate The Small

We often remind our students we want them to exhibit a growth mindset, all the while disconnecting ourselves with excuses on why we won't venture beyond our present reality. Let me encourage you to sit down and write a Top Ten "what if" list. What if time, money, or other limitations were not a factor? What would you do? Identify one that you could pursue over the next month; start small, challenge yourself to dive in and do it; maybe it is training for a marathon or taking a pottery class. Who knows! The important point is that will be the fuel for future passions; those small steps are something to recognize and celebrate! There is no magic in any one of these imperatives, but there is freedom. The freedom to experience life and not be a bystander of burnout. Drawing on the words of leadership giant John C. Maxwell, "You don't have to be great to get started, but you do have to start to be great."

Jeff Veal, Director of Professional Schools, Creator of @LeadUpNow and #LeadUpChat

---

CALL TO ACTION:

A friend and someone in my professional learning network, Greg Moffitt, told a group of leaders in the *Aspire Leadership Voxer Group* that leaders should not be viewed as "burnt-out candles." Instead, educators and leaders need to be viewed as propane tanks, a vessel that can be filled again and create fire at any point. Similar to a propane tank, leaders can start to feel empty. This is what you need to fill your vessel back up:

- Discover what you are passionate about
- Build a professional learning network to support you
- Create something that brings you joy
- Share it with other people

Education and leadership is a difficult job. If we continue to serve without finding inspiration from other avenues, we won't have anything else to give. Find your passion, fill your tank, and be on fire to help others.

QUESTIONS FOR DISCUSSION USING THE ASPIRE MODEL

- *Activate:* What passion project can you begin to find joy in outside of your profession?
- *Support:* Whose assistance do you need to learn from to be successful in this new project?
- *Persevere:* When you are tired from your long day, what systems are you putting in place to find the time and energy to work on your passion project?
- *Identify:* What areas are you passionate about in or out of education?
- *Reflect:* How is your passion project improving your personal and professional life?
- *Execute:* How can you share your passion project with other people?

Aspire Podcast Resource

Lead Up Now:
Featuring Jeff Veal

9

CREATIVITY IN LEADERSHIP

"Creative thinking is not a talent, it is a skill that can be learned. It empowers people by adding strength to their natural abilities which improves teamwork, productivity, and, where appropriate, profits."

— **EDWARD DE BONO**

A SKILL TO GROW

s an art teacher, I can't tell you how many times I heard students, parents, or other educators tell me, "Oh, I can't draw. I'll never be able to be an artist." It always bothered me because the comments meant that drawing isn't a skill you can grow on but a fixed God-given talent that people possess. I used to tell my students, "If I sat at a piano with no prior knowledge or experience, I wouldn't be able to play any music successfully. However, with time, teaching, and practice, I would be able to grow my musical skills and learn to play songs. Drawing is the same thing. You need to practice to get better."

For leaders, the same statement is true with creativity. When I hear an educator say, "Oh, I'm not very creative. I work on logistics and let other people develop creative ideas." Are you kidding? Educators are some of the most creative people on this entire earth. I have seen amazing wonders in the classroom with so few supplies, time, and resources. Similar to drawing or playing the piano, with practice, creativity is a skill that will grow.

I will admit, it was much easier to be creative with my ideas as an art teacher than an administrator. As a school leader, it is a far different practice. In the classroom, I was the ruler of my domain. I could take a risk and try new ideas without involving anyone else in the creative process. As a building leader, your decisions impact so many facets of the school and it would be unwise not to include others. When I first became an administrator, it took several years to feel comfortable offering up new ideas, inviting other people into the creative process, and pushing the boundaries of traditional practices. In this chapter, I want to share some examples and the processes of being creative as an educational leader.

PUT IDEAS IN THE MIXER

Before I share some of my experiences with creativity, I want you to know that the first thing we need to address is the vulnerability that comes with presenting new ideas. Regardless of the environment, you are at risk of judgment and criticism of your creative input. I learned this firsthand early in my leadership career. As a campus leadership group, we met on an issue that was occurring in athletics. For most of the meeting, I was listening to everyone's opinions on a solution and analyzing in my head the best option for resolution. Toward the end of the meeting, the principal asked me for my ideas on solving the problem. To the whole group, I identified what I deemed the issue was and provided my version of a solution. After I finished sharing with the group, a colleague quickly announced their displeasure with my ideas and stated, "What does he know he's only a first-year coach." The comment cut right through me. I felt I had given a lot of thought to my comments but I was quickly discredited by a peer. As an administrator now, I never want my staff to feel the same way in a meeting. If we are looking to solve a problem as a team, I want as many ideas out on the table as possible and I want everyone feeling safe to share their ideas. The more suggestions we collect, the better chance we have of finding the best solution.

My philosophy for brainstorming creative ideas has always stemmed from my time with my middle school soccer coach. During my seventh soccer season, my coach used to yell in practice and during games, "Put it in the mixer!" What he was trying to communicate was he wanted the outside wing player to cross the ball from the outside of the field to the center, about fifteen feet from the goalie box. His philosophy was that when you can get the ball in this area of the field, it was extremely dangerous for the other team. The coach would always say, "When it's in the mixer, you never know what's going to happen." As the year progressed and the coach hammered home this idea, we began to see great results from the strategy. Before his instruction, there was always a lot of fear of kicking the ball in this area of the field without the certainty of success. The philosophy and his communication were powerful because he allowed us to be aggressive, make mistakes, and capitalize on our teamwork.

I know you are probably wondering how kicking a ball to a certain area of the field translates to creativity. As a leader, I want you to put your creative thoughts and ideas "in the mixer." Kick your ideas around with people you trust, your teammates, and see what happens from the process. I promise that this collaboration process will produce great success. Here are a few examples of how I had a problem, threw the creative ideas "in the mixer," and our leadership team developed creative solutions.

The Creative Corner

As I was walking through classrooms and conducting a quick walk-through with the district's data collecting application, I noticed that I rarely witnessed students using technology during the lesson. At the time, our students were not one-to-one with laptops or devices, and each classroom only had a few desktop computers. After several months of witnessing little to no technology interaction, I created a Google Form to gather additional data on student and teacher technology use. I wanted to collect extensive information to find a true indicator of the problem. If the students were not using technology, why not? If the teachers are using technology in their lessons, how do we translate their practices to the students?

As I gathered data and had conversations with my teachers, it was evident that the teachers felt comfortable using technology to share information but they didn't know how to implement technology practices into the lesson for students to utilize in their learning. I believe technology knowledge is a key skill that students need to enhance their soft skills and be successful in future endeavors. As I assessed the data, it was clear that the students were rarely using technology or applications to research, construct projects, or collaborate on ideas. I needed to find a solution to this problem creatively. If I mandated that the teachers had to have the students use more technology, it would kill our collaborative culture and the teachers would not buy into the initiative. I needed to find a solution that empowered every educator in the building.

I met with the campus leadership team and I shared the technology data collected. We identified the areas of improvement, current logistical challenges, and practical solutions. As we went around the table sharing ideas, I shared an idea I had on a teacher-led professional development (PD) program called the "Creative Corner." The idea was that once a month we would have a voluntary PD session after school on an area of technology. The goal was to have a teacher share tips and tricks on how to engage students using a variety of applications, such as Flipgrid, Google Presentations, Chrome extensions, or Quizizz. The leadership team agreed that the teachers needed more tools to help the students use technology in the classroom to increase engagement, provide immediate feedback, and enhance student collaboration.

After the leadership meeting, we communicated to the staff about the program, started gathering teachers to present on various topics, and secured a location to meet. On the third Wednesday of the month, we conducted a voluntary Creative Corner PD, and we typically saw one-third of the staff each session. The Creative Corner gave our teachers a safe space to learn from their peers, ask questions, and explore the technology. And as a result, as I continued to complete technology walk-throughs throughout the year, we saw an increase in teacher and student technology use in the classroom.

Maker Morning

With the attempt to increase student technology use, we began to research technology resources for our students and how to provide opportunities for them to create beyond the classroom. At the time, many campuses around the country were constructing areas called "Maker-space." In a Makerspace, students are allowed to use a variety of tactile materials or technology tools to explore, build, and create new products. After reading several books and talking with several leaders on the theory and construction of a Makerspace, I was determined to build a similar environment on our campus.

There were several hurdles to overcome, such as funding, supplies, personnel, and space in the building. As I continued to gather information, it was evident that the supplies purchased by many schools were extremely expensive. Furniture alone was estimated to cost thousands of dollars. My principal and I began to write grants in hopes that we could gather additional funds for the construction of the creative space. In addition, we met with our district directors to propose our Makerspace in hopes of acquiring additional funds.

Our school didn't have many open areas available and it was difficult to find a space for our students to use. After searching the building, we decided the only logical space would be in the library. Our librarian had retired during the summer and we wanted to hire someone who had a similar vision for our Makerspace. We began interviewing candidates and found a wonderful librarian who was passionate about having the library as a learning space with a variety of resources. The librarian's excitement and dedication to the Makerspace were exactly what I needed to get the project off the ground. Now that we found the space and location, we refocused on the finances and supplies needed to allow students to create. The district approved our proposal and provided us with enough money to buy a variety of laptops, technology accessories, and other materials. In addition to the money we received from the district, we also were provided a grant from a technology company that provided our school with four large SMARTboards; two were mounted to the walls and two were portable. We didn't have enough funds to purchase furniture but since the Makerspace was in the library, we were able to piece together enough workspaces to accommodate our students.

Once we had the area of the library constructed, we began to advertise the Makerspace to our students. Our amazing librarian had a creative idea to open the library every Tuesday and Thursday morning to allow the students to explore the materials and technology, which was named "Maker Mornings." With each session, our librarian would provide a lesson on an application, technology tool, or hardware to teach the students how to use the materials in the space. The students were not required to use the tools taught that morning; however, the knowledge was beneficial for those who continued to come into the space to create. The Makerspace was very popular with our students and the library was packed every Tuesday and Thursday mornings.

ENHANCING THE CREATIVE CULTURE WITH COLLABORATION

Creativity is not meant to be a task conducted alone. It requires a team of individuals who have different talents, viewpoints, and experiences. If you notice, the examples I provided did not consist of me finding the problem, determining the solution, implementing the action steps, and continuing the practice alone. It required a team of people who collaborated to find a creative solution. As a leader, here are a few suggestions to enhance the creative culture in your building.

Ask for Suggestions

Throughout my time as an educator, from a paraprofessional to an administrator, I have seen many decisions made by leaders without the input of others within the building. I can't think of one example where this strategy was successful. To be effective as a creative leader, we need the assistance of others, but we can't assume the suggestions will come without a prompt. Ask for suggestions. Ask for feedback from your leadership team. Ask your staff to think differently than they have before.

Say Yes to Crazy Ideas

In my experience, most educators are used to hearing the word "no" —so much so that many teachers won't share creative ideas with their administrators. As leaders, we need to get out of the way of good and crazy ideas to allow for the growth of our teacher's creativity. Too often, we squash a creative idea due to the logistics of the project instead of focusing on the wonderful and fruitful possibilities of the end product.

Ownership of Ideas

When ideas are presented and agreed upon, it is important to give credit and praise to the person who has shared the creative idea. However, we can't stop there. We need to provide an opportunity for the person to take ownership of their ideas and progress with leading or partnering in the solution. By bringing the person with the creative idea along in the process, it builds a culture of empowerment, ingenuity, and leadership. It's one thing to have an idea but it's a completely different experience to construct the idea into reality.

———

Open the Door to Creativity
By Allyson Apsey

Creativity is a leadership art form. Creativity is the ability to see beyond what is, into what could be. It is not necessarily making up ideas from scratch. Creativity can be looking at someone else's way of doing things and figuring out how to make it work at your school. Creativity does not take a genius. It takes space and time. With school leadership, space and time are not always easily found, especially for early-career leaders.

As a veteran principal, over the years, the space for creativity in my professional life has widened. This occurs as leaders have more experience, confidence, and a broader knowledge base. It's the same with teachers—in the first year in a new grade level, teachers paddle to keep their heads afloat with all the new content coming at them. In the second year in that same grade level, a little space opens up for inserting creativity into student learning. The room for creativity continues to grow as each year progresses. It is the same with leadership, yet there is good news. That process can be hastened with deliberate effort.

How might aspiring school leaders or early-career principals make space for creativity, without waiting for it to be naturally created in the progression of their career?

Develop a file of ideas to consider: An aspiring leader will be inundated with creative ideas while collaborating with other leaders or simply perusing social media. When we are in the "doggy-paddle to stay alive" mode, great ideas coming at us are not lifelines. Instead, creative ideas can feel like anchors, things we want to make happen but have no capacity for at the time. Instead of avoiding social media or allowing the creativity of others to drown you, you must put the ideas away to consider at a designated time. Maybe you carve out a couple of hours on Sunday morning for dreaming, or you schedule a half-day once per month.

Take it one idea at a time: Information comes at us at an alarming speed. There is no way we could ever act upon all the great ideas that come our way. Whenever you designate time to get creative, make sure you walk out of that session with one or two specific ideas to integrate right away. You can leave the other ideas for consideration at another time. Don't worry, they will be there when you are ready for them.

Create an "Innovation Team": In my early years as a school leader, I made the mistake of doing it alone. I thought I was supposed to have all the answers. Looking back, I see how faulty my thinking was. Working in teams within a school not only takes the burden of creativity off the leader's back, but also empowers the team to have their voices heard and acted upon. Consider creating an "Innovation Team" whose sole purpose is to get creative—to see beyond what is, into what could be.

Above all else, take care of yourself. If we feel strong and powerful, we can take on the world. If we feel weak and constantly overwhelmed, even the smallest problems can seem insurmountable. All of us need adequate rest, healthy food, exercise, and fresh air. But, you guys, leaders need a healthy lifestyle even more. Supporting and uplifting staff AND students AND families is a big job. It is no wonder the weight on our shoulders is heavy. We have to permit ourselves to prioritize our wellness every step of the way. Not only does that help open the door to creativity, but it also helps us better serve everyone around us, every day.

Allyson Apsey, Elementary Principal, Author of *The Path to Serendipity* and *Through the Lens of Serendipity*

———

CALL TO ACTION:

Regardless of the position you hold, you have the ability to be creative. It's a skill that can grow with time, effort, and vulnerability. We need to focus on our ideas. By creating a habit of innovation and creativity in our organization, we can consistently establish a culture of unique solutions, instead of traditional and redundant practices. Similar to a sport or musical instrument, it requires repeated practice to improve the skill. Creativity is an essential skill for any leader to improve the culture in their building, enhance the learning environment, and solve difficult problems.

QUESTIONS FOR DISCUSSION USING THE ASPIRE MODEL

- *Activate:* What practices do you have in your organization to create a culture of creativity?
- *Support:* How will you guide and enhance the volume of ideas to develop creative solutions?
- *Persevere:* What crazy and innovative ideas are you able to support to change the creative culture of your organization?
- *Identify:* How will you determine an innovative and creative idea from your organization?
- *Reflect:* Have previous creative solutions been successful? If not, why?
- *Execute:* Once a creative idea is accepted, what needs to occur to make sure the implementation process is successful?

Aspire Podcast Resource

Serendipity in Education: Featuring Allyson Apsey

10

MINDSET OF A LION

"I never lose. I either win or I learn."

— *NELSON MANDELA*

everal years ago, I discovered an inspirational quote from Nelson Mandela on Twitter, which was written on a photograph of a lion walking through long safari grass. The quote and image immediately caught my attention, as they clearly depicted important characteristics of strength, grit, and growth mindset. As I reflected on the quote, it began to challenge my previous learning experiences, prior educational struggles, and my current beliefs as an administrator. Little did I know, the quote would become the motto I use as motivation for myself, my students, and my own children moving forward.

One afternoon, after a district meeting, I pulled into the parking lot of my school and parked. I turned the car off, pulled the keys out of the ignition, and remained sitting in the driver's seat. My mind and body were tired. The school year had taken a huge toll on me and I didn't even want to enter the building. As I slowly looked up, I saw a tree in the field near the school moving in a strange motion. As I looked further, I saw a teacher standing back looking up at the tree as it swayed back and forth. Without thinking further, I grabbed my bag, threw it around my shoulder, and walked to the tree. As I walked through the field, I passed the teacher, gave her a nod, and walked under the shaking tree.

Once I got to the trunk of the tree, the tree stopped moving. I looked up and saw one of our students sitting high up in the branches with a huge smile on his face. It was a student I worked with daily and I had built a positive relationship with during the school year.

I smiled back and said, "How are you doing?"

Jumping to another branch in the tree, the student said, "I'm fine. I just got overwhelmed in class and I needed to move around."

"Yeah, I totally get that. You picked a nice day to get outside."

"I always feel better when I climb trees."

"Well, if you're feeling better, I think it's time to go back to the building. Will you come down and walk back with me?"

Quickly, the student said, "Ok."

Before I knew it, the student was out of the tree and walking back to the school.

As we walked back, the teacher started walking beside me smiling and she said, "I'm so glad you came. I didn't know how I was going to get him out of that tree."

We both had a chuckle and I was able to get the student back into the building.

Looking back at that moment, it dawned on me that the student and I were feeling the same way that day. The only difference was he was in a tree and I was in my car. Neither of us had a clue how to deal with our issues at the moment; however, it was evident we both needed time to get away and process. Sitting in my car, I felt like a failure. I was questioning if I was making a difference at the school and If I could continue as a leader. Regardless of where you are in your leadership journey, you are going to have extremely difficult days ahead. There will be many days that you question your skills, feel as though you lost the fight, and are completely defeated. A few weeks later, still feeling beaten down, I saw the quote on Twitter from Nelson Mandela, which states:

"I never lose. I either win or I learn."

Now, You are probably asking, *why on earth are you ending your book by telling us how hard the job is?* The reason is simple: regardless of how good of a leader you are or how long you have been in your position, you will focus on your failures, weaknesses, and problems you have created and need to continue on your journey. This is exactly where I have been on multiple accounts, including the time I was sitting in the parking lot, not wanting to go back into the school. However, when I started focusing on the Nelson Mandela quote to fix my mindset, it made me reflect on my experiences and shift my outlook. Instead of constantly thinking of my missteps as failures, I started to view the trials and negative experiences as learning opportunities to become better. We have to remember that no one is perfect and it's ok to learn from our mistakes. Similar to the lion, we have to be strong and courageous to continue on through the trying times.

In addition to the shift in mindset and learning from our mistakes, I want you to use the ASPIRE model to help assist in your leadership decisions and enhance your learning experiences.

ACTIVATE. SUPPORT. PERSEVERE. IDENTIFY. REFLECT. EXECUTE.

A: Activate

It's easy to have great intentions, learn more about your craft, or brainstorm ideas. However, if you don't activate yourself, you will not be able to accomplish your goals. Even in the tough times, find the strength to act and pursue your dreams.

S: Support

It's incredibly important to find someone to guide and assist in your leadership experience. It doesn't matter how many years you have been a leader, you must find a mentor and a professional learning community to provide support, praise, and wisdom.

P: Persevere

As I have shared before, at some point, you are going to fail as a leader. Don't fixate on failure. Instead, use the mistakes as a learning experience. Some days you will win, and other days, you will learn.

I: Identify

Discover your strengths, values, passions, and convictions as a leader and utilize them to identify areas of improvement on your campus or your district.

R: Reflect

Reflection is one of the most important learning opportunities leaders possess to improve their skills and construct action plans. Make sure you designate time to process your previous actions and plan for your future.

E: Execute

Once we have gone through each of the steps in the ASPIRE Model, it is time to execute your plans. The preparation, guidance, and identification is complete and it's time to put your plans to work. Your students, teachers, and school community need your leadership.

By using the Aspire Model, you will be able to enhance your leadership skills, connect to inspirational people, and elevate yourself to accomplish your leadership goals. There are so many areas in education that need to be improved and problems that need to be solved. You have the power to make an immediate impact. Now, go ASPIRE to lead!

If you need anything to help your leadership journey, please connect with me on the following outlets:

Website: www.joshstamper.com
Twitter: @Joshua__Stamper
IG: @Joshua__Stamper
Voxer: @Joshua__Stamper
Facebook: @AspirePodcast
LinkedIn: Joshua Stamper
Email: Joshua@teachbetter.com

ACKNOWLEDGMENTS

I want to share my deep appreciation to those who have made an amazing impact on my life as a husband, father, leader, podcaster, and author. Thank you to my amazing wife, Leslie Stamper, for your constant support in my dreams and crazy ideas. Any success I have received only occurred because you were by my side. I am forever grateful for your love and dedication to our family. To my awesome kids, thank you for allowing me to work on this project during this past year. Your encouragement throughout the process has been extremely motivating and uplifting. To my mom, BJ Stamper, thank you for always believing in me, even when I didn't believe in myself.

Thank you to Sarah Thomas and EduMatch Publishing for providing me the opportunity to share the #AspireLead message through the publishing of this book and guiding me through this extensive process.

To Todd Nesloney, thank you for your friendship and the wonderful forward you provided for this book. Without your confidence in my leadership skills and providing opportunities to share, I wouldn't have explored all of these additional outlets and projects. You've had a huge impact on my growth as a leader, creator, and person.

I would like to thank Jeff Gargas and the Teach Better Team for their guidance and support for this book. Your wisdom and insight were instrumental in the development of this message.

Also, I would like to acknowledge and share my appreciation for my mentors. Sonja Pegram, Brant Perry, Ann Aston, Shurandia Holden, Christopher Tobler, and Robin Scott, thank you for your wisdom, coaching, encouragement, and shared knowledge over the years. Your influence shaped and molded me into the educational leader I am today.

Lastly, I want to thank my PLN. This has been a difficult and odd year, and with your support, I have been able to continue my growth as a leader. The Aspire podcast and this book would not exist without you. Thank you to the contributing authors and your inspiring words. Each of you has had a huge influence on my professional learning network and I am honored to be connected with you.

ABOUT THE AUTHOR

With an economic crash and professional uncertainty, Joshua went from using his creativity and innovative ideas as a graphic designer to inspiring students to use their imagination as an art teacher. Being unsuccessful as a student growing up, Joshua never thought he would be back in the classroom as a teacher and now as an administrator. The struggles as a student spawned a passion and desire to change the education model, push the boundaries of traditional learning, and explore new creative ideas.

Joshua has had the great pleasure of working as a middle school Assistant Principal for a North Texas School District for the past eight years, where he's been able to serve at four campuses and in two school districts. Before entering into administration, Joshua was a classroom

Art educator and athletic coach for six years working with students in grades six through eight.

In addition to his administrative position, Joshua is the host of Aspire: The Leadership Development Podcast, author, leadership coach, education presenter, and Podcast Network Manager for the Teach Better Team.

Joshua is married to Leslie and has five wonderful kids, Mila, Landon, Gabriel, Aden, and Elijah.

You can follow Joshua on social media @Joshua__Stamper and visit his website at joshstamper.com.

Bring Joshua to Your Organization or Event!
Contact Jeff Gargas at jeff@teachbetter.com for booking

PUBLISHING

CPSIA information can be obtained
at www.ICGtesting.com
Printed in the USA
FSHW021709170921
84824FS